Eels as Pets

A Complete Guide

Where to buy, species, aquarium, supplies, diet, care, tank setup, and more!

By Lolly Brown

Copyrights and Trademarks

All rights reserved. No part of this book may be reproduced or transformed in any form or by any means, graphic, electronic, or mechanical, including photocopying, recording, taping, or by any information storage retrieval system, without the written permission of the author.

This publication is Copyright © 2014. All products, graphics, publications, software and services mentioned and recommended in this publication are protected by trademarks. In such instance, all trademarks & copyright belong to the respective owners.

Disclaimer and Legal Notice

This product is not legal, medical, or accounting advice and should not be interpreted in that manner. You need to do your own due-diligence to determine if the content of this product is right for you. While every attempt has been made to verify the information shared in this publication, neither the author, neither publisher, nor the affiliates assume any responsibility for errors, omissions or contrary interpretation of the subject matter herein. Any perceived slights to any specific person(s) or organization(s) are purely unintentional.

We have no control over the nature, content and availability of the web sites listed in this book. The inclusion of any web site links does not necessarily imply a recommendation or endorse the views expressed within them. We take no responsibility for, and will not be liable for, the websites being temporarily unavailable or being removed from the internet.

The accuracy and completeness of information provided herein and opinions stated herein are not guaranteed or warranted to produce any particular results, and the advice and strategies, contained herein may not be suitable for every individual. Neither the author nor the publisher shall be liable for any loss incurred as a consequence of the use and application, directly or indirectly, of any information presented in this work. This publication is designed to provide information in regard to the subject matter covered.

Neither the author nor the publisher assume any responsibility for any errors or omissions, nor do they represent or warrant that the ideas, information, actions, plans, suggestions contained in this book is in all cases accurate. It is the reader's responsibility to find advice before putting anything written in this book into practice. The information in this book is not intended to serve as legal, medical, or accounting advice.

Foreword

Truthfully, the first "eel" I encountered – or thought I encountered – was a Kuhli Loach, a whole little pack of them, in fact, that my father brought home from the fish store. I was a late-in-life child, so my parents worked extra hard at making sure they did all the proper "kid" things with me. This included setting up an aquarium.

Of course, my Dad had difficulty with the term "small scale." Yes, we began with a nice little 10 gallon / 37.85 liter tank and within a matter of months had graduated to 120 gallons / 454.25 liters.

With his typical enthusiasm for projects, Dad acquired reference materials, studied water quality, pondered the merits of various filtration systems, and took to population management like an aquatic prison warden.

He archly warned Mother that her insistence on buying an angelfish was a mistake and when Neon Tetras started disappearing daily, he was proven correct.

The Kuhli Loaches, along with several large snails, were part and parcel of his "tank cleaning crew" plan. In the end, I think he and I enjoyed watching the snails and the "eels" more than the fish.

Kuhli Loaches love to hide, so more and more tank decorations were added for their specific use, including a tower with windows and passageways into which they

Foreword

would wedge their elongated bodies. They were, frankly, just plain fun and I can recall coming home from school in the afternoon and looking forward to seeing them each day.

I don't know if my parents intended the aquarium to be as educational as it was, or if they were just seeking to divert my all-too-active mind, but I never forgot the Kuhli Loaches, which are, technically, "eel-like" fish.

As I was researching this book, selecting species of eels to profile was difficult. The inclusion of some creatures, like the Saltwater Morays, was obvious, but it seemed that every time I thought my list was done, I'd run across another type of eel that someone, somewhere acquired and put in a tank.

I don't pretend that the creatures I discuss here are all the eels that can be kept in an aquarium environment. I have tried to cover the ones you are most likely to encounter, including some creatures that, though rare, can still be purchased.

Clearly eels are of high-interest value in a tank, but almost all present specific husbandry challenges. Most of the largest eels are carnivores and cannot be used in reef tanks, but even the benign Spotted Garden Eel is a real estate hog, requiring 1 square foot / 0.09 square meter of open sandy substrate per eel.

In addition to profiling various types of eels, I also provide an overview of considerations necessary to creating an

Foreword

underwater environment. For experienced aquarists, this information may not be as relevant, but if you are thinking of starting a tank for the express purpose of raising eels, you must understand that it's not just a matter of throwing some fish in a glass box full of water.

For one thing, have you even considered the issue of volume as it translates to weight? A 180-gallon / 681.37-liter tank weighs 1,440 lbs. / 653.17 kg. You're not going to just plunk that down anywhere in your house.

My intent here is to introduce you to the world of aquarium eels and to the basic requirements of designing an environment for them. Once you know the type of eel in which you are interested, you should be able to easily determine the equipment to acquire and install.

I strongly urge you to find a community of fellow enthusiasts as a resource. Having a mentor or mentors in the aquarium hobby is greatly to your advantage. There are many including:

- Monster Fish Keepers at www.monsterfishkeepers.com
- The Reef Tank at www.thereeftank.com
- The Age of Aquariums at www.aquahobby.com
- Fish Tank Forums at www.fishtankforums.com
- Tropical Fish Keeping at www.tropicalfishkeeping.com

Connecting with people actively keeping eels and other

Foreword

large fish and learning from their experience will greatly increase your chances of successfully raising these beautiful and exotic animals.

Regardless of the scale on which you keep true eels or eel-like fish, these creatures, with their snake-like bodies and unusual behaviors add visual appeal and high interest to any tank and are thus, some of the most popular species in the hobby.

Acknowledgments

I would like to express my gratitude towards my family, friends, and colleagues for their kind co-operation and encouragement which helped me in completion of this book.

I would like to express my special gratitude and thanks to my loving husband for his patience, understanding, and support.

My thanks and appreciations also go to my colleagues and people who have willingly helped me out with their abilities.

Additional thanks to my children, whose love and care for our family pets inspired me to write this book.

Table of Contents

Table of Contents

Foreword 1

Acknowledgments 5

Table of Contents... 7

Chapter 1 – Understanding Aquarium "Eels" 11

    Characteristics of True Eels 12

        Using the Term "Eel" 13

    Buying Aquarium Eels 14

Chapter 2 – Saltwater Moray Eels...................................... 17

    Dragon Moray Eel 19

    Snowflake Moray Eel... 21

    Zebra Moray Eel... 24

    Whitemouth Moray Eel 27

    Chainlink Moray Eel.. 29

    Other Moray Species.. 30

        Dwarf or Golden Dwarf Moray 30

        Golden Moray Eel 31

        Fire Coral Eel 32

        Tessalata Moray Eel 33

    Miscellaneous Morays 34

Chapter 3 – Spiny Eels... 37

    Tire Track Eel.. 37

Table of Contents

Fire Eel 38

Half-Banded Spiny Eel 39

Peacock Eel 41

Chapter 4 – Eel-Like Fish 43

Wolf Eel or Carpet Eel Snakelet 43

Kuhli Loach 45

Java Loach 46

Panther Loach or Platinum Line Loach 47

Weather Loach or Dojo Loach 48

White Ribbon Eel or Ghost Eel 49

Rope Fish 51

Electric Eel 52

Chapter 5 – Miscellaneous Eels 55

The Purple Spaghetti Eel 55

The Rubber Eel 56

The Spotted Garden Eel 57

The Marble Swamp Eel 60

American Eel 61

Chapter 6 – Creating Aquatic Environments ... 65

Weight Matters – A Lot! 65

What Can Your Floors Take? 66

Finding the Strongest Room 67

Table of Contents

Is That All I Need to Know? 68
Tanks by Type 69
The Basics of Water Chemistry 70
   pH 70
   Water Hardness 71
   Specific Gravity 71
Cycling: Establishing Viable Water 72
Dispelling the Major Myth 73
Chapter 7 – Creating and Keeping a Moray Tank 75
Form and Function 75
Moray Habitats 76
   Volume vs. Configuration 78
   Glass vs. Acrylic 80
   Lighting 80
   Temperature 81
   Substrate 82
   Tank Structures 82
   Security Precautions 84
Water Quality and Health 84
Feeding Time 85
Issues of Pure Aesthetics 88
   The Golden Ratio 88

Table of Contents

    The Rule of Thirds 89

    Avoid the Symmetry Trap 89

Chapter 8 – Health Considerations 91

    Introductory Quarantine 91

    External Parasites 92

    White Spot or Ick 94

    Internal Parasites 95

    Injuries 96

    Fungal and Bacterial Infections 97

    Malnutrition 97

    Tumors 98

    Euthanasia 99

Chapter 9 – Frequently Asked Questions 101

Afterword 106

Relevant Websites 109

    Eel-Specific Links 109

    General Aquarium Links 110

Glossary 113

Index 120

Chapter 1 – Understanding Aquarium "Eels"

Chapter 1 – Understanding Aquarium "Eels"

The long, snake-like fish kept by enthusiasts in both fresh and saltwater aquariums that are commonly referred to as "eels" may be true eels from the order of *Anuilliformes*, or any one of a number of "eel-like" fishes.

Anuilliformes are elongated fish. They include members of the family *Anguillidae* like the American Eel and the European Eel, or those found in the family *Moringuidae* like Worm Eels and Spaghetti Eels.

Spiny Eels, however, are actually "eel-like" fish. They belong to the *Mastacembelidae* family. Even the well-known Electric Eel (*Electrophorus electricus*) is actually a Naked-

Chapter 1 – Understanding Aquarium "Eels"

Backed Knifefish (family *Gymnotidae*.) And Rubber Eels aren't eels or fish, but amphibiains!

Basically, just because it *looks* like an eel, doesn't mean it actually *is* an eel.

Characteristics of True Eels

All true eels have a laundry list of readily identifiable characteristics including:

- elongated bodies
- a snake-like appearance
- no pelvic fins
- no pectoral fins
- no gill cover openings
- no scales
- continuous dorsal and anal fins
- locomotion via flowing, undulating strokes
- mucous covering for protection against abrasions

Moray eels, in particular, have lateral line pores on their heads. This allows them to hide in crevices and caves with just their heads sticking out while still being able to sense movement in the surrounding water.

In many cases the creatures characterized as "eel-like" fish have none of these special adaptions, but they do have elongated bodies. Because making these distinctions can be very difficult for all but the experts, I am choosing to go with more simplified language.

Chapter 1 – Understanding Aquarium "Eels"

Using the Term "Eel"

For the purposes of this text, I will discuss "aquarium eels" as a group of eels, fishes, and even amphibians that share the common characteristic of having long, snake-like bodies. These creatures may live in salt or fresh water. Most consume similar diets, and are intelligent fish with a penchant for staging escapes.

If there is one rule of thumb with which to begin your interest in keeping eels it is this: ***cover your tank, tightly!***

The following chapters will provide descriptions of the most popular eels kept by aquarists and look at specialized aspect of their husbandry including the design of tunnels and hiding spaces.

While this book is not intended as a "how to" aquarium book per se, I think it's important to provide an overview of some of this material, especially for those readers still sitting on the fence about whether or not to take up this pastime.

Be forewarned. Designing and keeping an underwater environment, especially one you have created around a showcase species like a prized eel, can be an all-consuming passion – and an expensive one.

Many of these eels require huge tanks, so large in fact that you may even find yourself reinforcing the floors in your house to accommodate the weight of the water.

Chapter 1 – Understanding Aquarium "Eels"

For this reason, many eel enthusiasts are forced to dial back their expectations and settle for incorporating smaller "eel like" fish in their tanks. This does not have to be seen as a compromise, however, as many of these creatures are both beautiful and intriguing.

To begin with, however, we will look at some of the largest and most popular eels kept by saltwater aquarists, the moray eels. They are all aggressive carnivores and cannot simply be introduced into any existing saltwater tank without serious considerations of population management.

Buying Aquarium Eels

By and large, the various "eel-like" fish are not difficult to find and can be obtained from any good aquarium store. For larger and rare eels, you may find yourself shopping online.

As an example, Live Aquaria at www.liveaquaria.com offered about half a dozen species at the time of this writing in mid-2014. Of those, four were marked "seasonal" or "out of stock."

The site offers a "100% arrive alive, stay alive" 14-day guarantee with the option for a refund or account credit. They are located in Rhinelander, Wisconsin. The company cannot ship to Hawaii, APO addresses, post office boxes, Puerto Rico, U.S. territories, or internationally.

Always read the shipping policies of any entity with which

Chapter 1 – Understanding Aquarium "Eels"

you deal. In most cases, you or someone else will need to be waiting to accept the shipment and care for the eel. Making the best arrangements will likely necessitate a telephone call.

In the UK, look at Tropical Fish by Post at www.tropicalfishbypost.co.uk. They deliver in England, Wales, Scotland, and Ireland. At the time of this writing, the site listed three species, but only the Tire Track Eel was in stock.

Chapter 2 – Saltwater Moray Eels

Chapter 2 – Saltwater Moray Eels

Worldwide there are 15 genera in the family *Muraendae* to which the moray eels belong. This accounts for a total of 200 species. Of those, about a dozen could be raised in a home aquarium. Only five of those, however, can be safely housed with other fish, and this is still a highly conditional assertion.

- Dragon Moray Eel
- Snowflake Moray Eel
- Zebra Moray Eel
- Whitemouth Moray Eel
- Chainlink Moray Eel

The saltwater moray eels are all highly aggressive carnivores. They even look menacing, holding their mouths open not as a means of intimidation, but as a physiological necessity.

A moray eel's mouth must be open so that muscles in the gill cavity that are attached to the lower jawbone can draw water through the oral cavity and over the gills. The result of this very practical arrangement, however, is an especially fierce appearance augmented by the creature's pointed fangs that look more than ready to do battle.

Although they are formidable hunters, moray eels are also shy bottom dwellers that require adequate spaces to hide. They possess lateral line pores on their heads that allow them to lie in wait with their heads extended sensing

Chapter 2 – Saltwater Moray Eels

vibrations in the water around them. This ability, combined with their superb sense of smell compensates for limited vision, while the creature's wedge-shaped head allows it to extract prey from almost any hiding place.

When an eel senses prey entering its perimeter, the eel moves its head from side to side to more accurately find and identify the approaching scent. To confirm their selections, morays eels often tap or bump potential prey with their snouts, using taste and touch receptors in their nose and lips.

In captivity, moray eels are skilled escape artists, and all must be kept in covered tanks. The species most commonly kept by enthusiasts grow to an average maximum length of 3 feet / 0.91 meters, except the Whitemouth, which can reach 4 feet / 1.22 meters.

Chapter 2 – Saltwater Moray Eels

Moray eels are notoriously difficult to feed in captivity, and are prone to periods of hibernation. Of the five species listed earlier in this chapter, only the Zebra Moray Eel can be housed in a community tank with any great degree of success.

Dragon Moray Eel

Other common names: Leopard Moray Eel, Japanese Dragon Moray Eel

The Dragon Moray Eel (*Enchelycore pardalis*) is especially distinctive for the horns (exterior nostrils) that grow directly over the eyes creating the dragon-like appearance from which the species draws its name.

The creature's native range extends from Hawaii to southern Japan and south to the Indo-Pacific region. A predatory bottom dweller, it requires plenty of hiding places.

Because Dragon Eels do not tolerate deep, cold water, they rarely swim below 164 feet / 50 meters in the ocean. They are commonly found on living reefs, in caves, under overhangs, amid sunken wreckage, and in intertidal zones along rocky coastlines.

Physically stunning, Dragon Eels experience changes in both their colors and markings as they mature. Adults are primarily bright yellow with unusual patterns of lines and spots on the body in hues of orange/red, black, and white.

Chapter 2 – Saltwater Moray Eels

The dorsal fin is covered in either contiguous blotches or vertical bars.

When fully mature, captive specimens generally fall in a range of 30-33 inches / 0.76-0.83 meters, while their wild counterparts are often as long as 3 feet / 0.91 meters.

Clearly, based on size alone, a Dragon Eel requires a large tank. Experts agree that while a 100-gallon / 378.5-liter tank is an acceptable minimum, 125 gallons / 473 liters is preferable.

Specific water quality parameters for successful husbandry include:

- pH: 8.1-8.4
- Specific Gravity: 1.020-1.025
- Temperature: 72-78 F (22-26 C)

Most captive deaths in eel species are a direct result of either poor water quality or stress. When first introduced to a tank, a Dragon Moray will typically go into complete hiding. Leave the creature alone! This solitary acclimatization is crucial.

Because this is a highly aggressive species with large teeth and a bottom jaw that cannot close due to its curvature, the Dragon Eel presents challenges when housed with other types of marine life including other eel species.

For this reason, it's best to keep only one Dragon Eel at a

Chapter 2 – Saltwater Moray Eels

time and only in a tank specifically designed for other aggressive species including Groupers, Triggers, Snappers, Puffers, Lionfishes, and Hawks.

(Please note that some Dragon Eel enthusiasts think this species is a better candidate for a quiet reef tank since the amount of waste produced by other fish can be a problem given the species' need for superior water quality. Top-notch filtration and protein skimming are a must with Dragon Morays.)

As a carnivorous hunter, the Dragon Eel prefers to hunt and dine on live foods; therefore it can be difficult to feed in captivity. Your best food choices are live squid, shrimp, crab, and small fish offered on a feeding stick.

Even in the best-case scenario, however, individuals will only eat a couple of times a week. It is not unusual (nor a cause for alarm) for a newly introduced eel to go several weeks without feeding at all. The species also goes through periods of "hibernation," during which it hides constantly and refuses all food.

Dragon Moray Eels are expensive. Depending on the size at purchase, expect to pay $1000+ / £592+.

Snowflake Moray Eel

Other Common Names: Snowflake Moray, Clouded Moray, Nebulous or Starry Moray.

Chapter 2 – Saltwater Moray Eels

The Snowflake Moray Eel (*Echidna nebulosa*) has a white or cream body with branching black blotches that contain one or two yellow spots. There are also yellow markings on the head and the eyes are yellow.

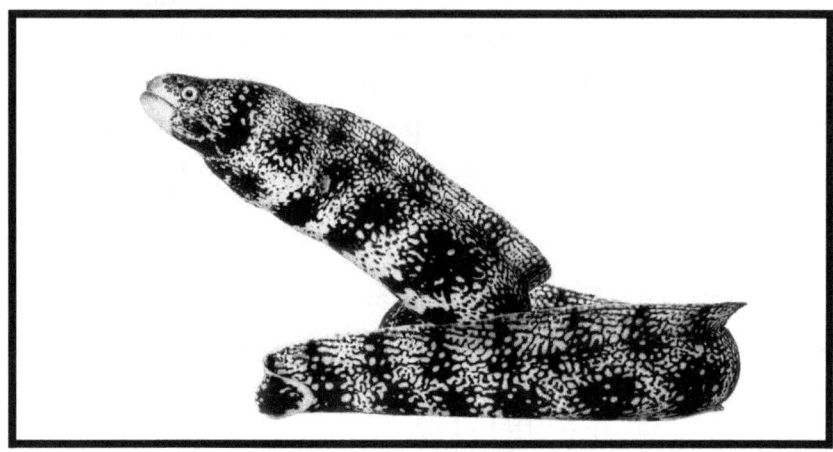

The Snowflake's native range extends southward from Hawaii to Australia and west through the Indo-Pacific and into the East Indies as well as across the Indian Ocean and along the coast of Africa.

The creatures are commonly found in reef lagoons and on reef slopes. They are not a deep water fish, rarely going below 98.4 feet / 30 meters.

They also frequent tidal zones and may be seen slithering out of the water at low tide to feed on shore crabs and other small crustaceans, including mantis shrimp and small bony fish as well as small cephalopods.

Snowflakes are considered to be one of the most beautiful

Chapter 2 – Saltwater Moray Eels

of the morays, a fact that contributes to their popularity with aquarists. They can reach 3 feet / 0.91 meters in length, but typically stay within 12-24 inches / 0.30-0.60 meters in captivity and therefore can be housed in a 75-gallon / 283.9-liter tank.

Although Snowflake Eels are considered less aggressive than other saltwater morays, they can become combative at feeding time, even going so far as to take a bite out of a passing fish. This is why the use of a feeding stick is recommended.

Using this rigid tube, the food item can be placed within inches of the eel, thus controlling the extent of its potential excited aggression. In fact, Snowflake eels that are trained to take food from a stick tend to wait for their meal to be offered to them.

Snowflake eels have blunt teeth, which they use to crush their prey. For this reason they are sometimes referred to as a "pebble-toothed moray." In captivity, they especially like crustaceans, but will also eat fish. Over time, and with patience, they can be taught to accept a wide variety of fresh and frozen foods including: clams, crabs, shrimp, scallops, and various fish meats.

Typically Snowflake eels will eat several times a week, which helps them to ignore the potential of other tank inhabitants becoming tasty snacks. Like other moray eels, the Snowflake will often go into a period of hibernation during which it refuses to eat for several weeks.

Chapter 2 – Saltwater Moray Eels

This species should only be kept with other aggressive fish, preferably those that are larger than the eel itself, which will discourage any predation. They are not appropriate for a reef tank. The necessary water parameters are:

- pH: 8.1-8.4
- Specific Gravity: 1.020-1.025
- Temperature: 74-82ºF (23.3-27.7C)

Snowflake Eels are superb escape artists and due to their slender build, can get through gaps that would stop other eels. Tight tank security is required to keep this species.

In comparison to other eels, the Snowflake Moray is relatively inexpensive, selling for $30-$60 depending on size (£17.82-£35.64)

Zebra Moray Eel

The Zebra Moray Eel (*Gymnomuraena zebra*) is one of the more docile of the morays. Since it is not normally aggressive with smaller fish, this reclusive bottom dweller can be kept in a community fish tank, but will need at least 4 inches / 10.16 cm of substrate.

A Zebra Eel will stay hidden most of the day with nothing more than its head sticking out, but over time will become comfortable enough to emerge and look for food even when the tank lights are on.

A native of the warm waters of the Pacific and Indian

Chapter 2 – Saltwater Moray Eels

Oceans and the Red Sea, Zebra Morays inhabit coral and rock reefs. The name "zebra" is well chosen for this striking eel with its dark brown body circled in thin white bands. Captive adults can reach a maximum length of 3 feet / 0.91 meters, but will do well in a 75-gallon / 283.9-liter tank or larger.

The Zebra Eel uses its pebble-like, blunt teeth to crush crustaceans, which are its favorite meal, but many small items are swallowed whole. When first introduced to a tank, Zebras frequently refuse to eat, but can be enticed with live feeder crabs.

In a home aquarium, this will sound like a holiday nutcracker when the eel holds down the crab with the coils of its body and snaps off the claws.

Juvenile Zebra Morays adapt more readily to aquarium life, and can be acclimated to frozen items including crab, clam, scallop, shrimp, fish, and squid meat. Since Zebras must be

Chapter 2 – Saltwater Moray Eels

fed several times a week, it's a good idea to get them accustomed early in life to a variety of acceptable foods.

Be aware, however, that a Zebra Eel, like others of its kind, can enter a hibernation period lasting several weeks during which time it will eat nothing. Individuals may become aggressive at meal times necessitating the use of a feeding stick, and their preference is to hunt or be fed behind reef structures rather than out in the open.

Specific water parameters for Zebra Moray Eels include:

- pH: 8.1-8.4
- Specific Gravity: 1.020-1.025
- Temperature: 72-78 F (22.2-25.5 C)

Due to their shy and reclusive nature, they should be provided with ample rock structures in which to hide. They are NOT, however, considered safe for reef tanks since they will happily snack on ornamental crustaceans and shelled invertebrates.

As Zebra Morays age, they become much thicker in the body and very muscular, which contributes to their more or less clumsy behavior. Any structures you place in the tank have to be large and strong to withstand a Zebra blundering about, especially at feeding time.

Zebra Moray Eels are moderately priced in a range of $120-$300 (£71.28-£178.22) depending on size at purchase.

Chapter 2 – Saltwater Moray Eels

Whitemouth Moray Eel

Other Common Names: Guinea Moray Eel, Guineafowl Moray, Painted Moray, Puhi'onio, Spotted Eel, Spotted Moray, Turkey Moray

The Whitemouth Moray Eel (*Gymnothorax meleagris*) is indigenous to the Indo-Pacific. Its preference for shallow water is so pronounced, it can often be found at depths of just 3 feet / 0.91 meters in lagoons, intertidal zones, rock-strewn flats, and seaward reefs.

Even in captivity, adults can grow to a maximum length of 4 feet / 1.21 meters. For this reason the recommended minimum tank size for the species is 200 gallons / 757 liters.

Chapter 2 – Saltwater Moray Eels

The brown to yellow-brown body is liberally covered in white spots edged in a dark tone. The inside of the mouth and tip of the tail are white, while the gill openings are surrounded by black blotches. The upper jaw holds two enlarged canine teeth.

The species can be kept with other morays, but only in very large tanks. Whitemouth Eels will, however, eat ornamental shrimp and smaller fish.

Typically the species should be fed twice a week on live, fresh, or frozen fish and crustacean meat. It is not unusual for these eels to "hibernate" for as long as two weeks at a time and to eat nothing during that period.

Provide a Whitemouth Eel with plenty of hiding places, but do not try to keep them in a reef tank. Specific water parameters should be:

- pH: above 8.0
- Specific Gravity: 1.022 – 1.025
- Temperature: 72-82 F (22.2-27.7 C)

Whitemouth Morays are very prone to jumping right out of the tank, so extra vigilance is required when opening and closing the lid.

Depending on the size at purchase, Whitemouth Morays are generally priced from $150 to $175 (£89.67-£104.61).

Chapter 2 – Saltwater Moray Eels

Chainlink Moray Eel

Other Common Names: Chain Moray

The Chainlink Moray Eel, (*Echidna catenata*) is indigenous to the warm waters off Brazil where it lives in rock and coral reefs. As juveniles, these eels are banded in green with alternating yellow stripes. Pattern and coloration varies widely by individual. As the eels age, their color and markings tend to become lighter and run together.

They are reclusive, nocturnal predators feeding primarily on crabs that they pursue with such avidity they will even leave the water and come onto shore to capture them. Chainlink Moray Eels adapt surprisingly well to aquarium life so long as they have adequate hiding places and are allowed enough time to acclimate themselves.

Since a Chainlink Moray can reach a maximum size of 2 feet 6 inches, a tank 125 gallons / 473.18 liters or larger is required.

In the beginning, a diet of live fiddler or blue crabs will be required, but over time this species will accept prepared foods and can learn to take chunks offered on a feeding stick. Adults need 2-3 meals per week.

Suggested water parameters include:

- pH 8.1-8.4
- sg 1.020-1.025

Chapter 2 – Saltwater Moray Eels

- temperature 72-78 F / 22.2-25.5 C

The typical size at sale for a Chainlink Eel is 6-8 inches / 15.24-20.32 cm at a price of $50 / £29.79.

Other Moray Species

Although these five moray species are the ones most typically seen in the hobby today, there are other species that crop up from time to time, including the Dwarf or Golden Dwarf Moray, which grows to a maximum length of only 10 inches / 25.4 cm, making it a desirable addition for enthusiasts of "nano" reef tanks (approximately 15 gallons / 56.78 liters.)

Dwarf or Golden Dwarf Moray

The Golden Dwarf Moray (*Gymnothorax melatremus*) is indigenous to the Indo-Pacific and varies in coloration from yellow to dark yellow or orange. Like all morays, they enjoy rocky hiding places and are skilled at escaping from tanks.

Although tiny in comparison to the massive morays described earlier in the chapter, this creature is still a carnivore, preferring silversides, clams, and pieces of fish, but generally agreeable to frozen foods.

The Golden Dwarf Moray is not overtly an aggressive and will cohabitate peacefully even with small fish. It does best in stable, well-maintained water in a temperature range of

Chapter 2 – Saltwater Moray Eels

72-82 F / 22-28 C.

Although desirable for its size and agreeable nature, this is an extremely rare eel. When a company does acquire a few specimens for sale, they disappear quickly.

The Golden Dwarf Moray is difficult to locate and may cost as much as $400 / £239.30.

Golden Moray Eel

The Golden Moray Eel (*Gymnothorax miliaris*), sometimes referred to as the Goldentail Moray, is another species that occasionally shows up in the hobby. Technically it is the same species as the Fire Coral Eel, but in the rare yellow

Chapter 2 – Saltwater Moray Eels

coloration.

Indigenous to reefs off South America, it is also popular for its relatively small adult size of just 2 feet 3 inches / 0.69 meters when fully grown.

There are several color variations, ranging from speckled brown and gold to bright yellow with the brighter shades being the most rare and most desirable.

This moray dines on crustaceans and occasionally small fish, so care should be taken when picking potential tank mates. Smaller species will likely not fare well in the company of a Golden Moray Eel.

Only highly experienced aquarists should attempt to raise this species since the Golden Moray is capable of inflicting severe bites. A minimum 125 gallon / 473 liter tank is recommended with the following water paramters:

- pH 8.1-8.4
- sg 1.020-1.025
- temperature 72-78 F / 22.2-25.5 C

At purchase, Golden Moray Eels are 4-18 inches / 10.16-45.72 cm and cost $700-$800 / £420-£480.

Fire Coral Eel

As mentioned above, the Fire Coral Eel is the same species as the Golden Moray Eel, but it is black with gold spots covering the body. Otherwise, all of the care parameters are identical to those provided for the Golden Moray Eel, but this is a much more common variant of the species, selling in a range of $190-$230 / £114-£138.

Tessalata Moray Eel

Other Common Names: Laced Moray, Leopard Moray, Tesselate Moray, or Honeycomb Moray

The Tessalata Moray Eel (*Gymnothorax favagineus*) is a handsome specimen, displaying a brown leopard pattern over a yellow white background.

The species is indigenous to the Indo-Pacific, East Africa to Papua New Guinea, north to the tip of Japan, and south to Australia. They live at depths of as much as 148 feet / 45 meters.

Typically they prefer crevices in reefs, and need aquascaping with sufficient caves and niches to completely shelter their bodies.

It should be noted that Tessalata Moray Eels produce an especially high bio-load, necessitating the need for strong mechanical and biological filtration.

This species can be kept in an aquarium, but grows to a maximum size of 5 feet 8 inches / 1.8 meters, thus requiring 180 gallons / 681.37 liters at minimum.

Chapter 2 – Saltwater Moray Eels

Most experts agree that the tank should have a width of at least 2 feet (0.6 meters) front to back and a length of six feet (1.83 meters).

Tessalata Morays are highly aggressive and should only be kept with other large aggressive species. Their level of aggression increases markedly at feeding time. Appropriate meaty foods include raw shrimp, squid, krill, clam, and mussel.

They will accept food offered on a feeding stick and typically are not reticent about feeding when first introduced to a tank problem, a behavior common among many other morays.

Tessalata Morays are generally 6-18 inches / 15.24-45.72 cm at purchase and sell for $150 to $200 / £90-£120.

Miscellaneous Morays

Although less popular or more difficult to obtain, you may also see the following species from time to time in the hobby:

- **Barred Moray** (*Echidna polyzana*), an eel indigenous to the Red Sea and eastern Africa east to Hawaii. Maximum adult size 30 inches / 0.76 meters. Requires a 75-gallon tank / 284-liter. Crustaceans are the primary diet for this pale to charcoal gray eel banded in bars of white or cream. They are active tank inhabitants and must be placed with fish that

Chapter 2 – Saltwater Moray Eels

will not harass them. These eels will not thrive with fast moving or "nippy" fish like angels, tangs, triggers, or wrasses.

- **Abbott's Moray** (*Gymnothorax eurosus*) reaches a maxium adult size of 24-30 inches / 0.60-0.76 meters and can be kept in a 75-gallon / 284-liter tank. They are strictly nocturnal and are indiscriminate carnivores. Colorations range from purple to light brown with golden to yellow-brown freckling. Without lots of rockwork and retreats built into the aquascaping of a tank, this species will not feel safe and may starve to death. Should be kept alone or with docile species only.

- The **Blackspotted Moray** (*Gymnothorax favagineus*) is a mammoth among the morays, reaching a gigantic size of 10 feet / 3.04 meters, which demands 200 gallons / 757 liters at minimum. It is a top reef predator, and a truly beautiful specimen with a white to yellow base color covered in irregular brown to black spots. It is sometimes referred to as the Honeycomb Moray. This species has a double row of razor sharp teeth and is capable of inflicting a painful bite. Definitely a species for an experienced aquarist only.

- The **Fimbriated Moray** (*Gymnothorax fimbriatus*) is a native of the Indo-Pacific that seldom grows larger than 30-32 inches / 0.76-0.81 meters. Requires a 75-gallon tank / 284-liter. It is a reef eel that also favors

Chapter 2 – Saltwater Moray Eels

tidal flats, overhangs, seaward ledges, mangrove tangles, grassy sandbars, and shipwrecks. The base color is light tan to a yellow-green and is accented by random dark spots. This species has a tendency to be finicky in captivity and should not be exposed to more than 8-10 hours of light per day.

- The **Yellow-Edged Moray** (*Gymnothorax flavimarginatus*) is another massive moray, reaching 6 feet / 1.8 meters in length in captivity, and 6.5 feet / 1.9 meters in the wild. It is widespread throughout the Indo-Pacific region and is a resident of shallow to deep water, from tidal pools to depths of 525 feet / 160 meters. They are powerful and opportunistic predators. The base color is yellowish overlaid with a dense mass of brown to black spots and speckles. Red eyes sit above the elongated snout flanked by bulging jaw muscles. The species requires at least a 500-gallon aquarium, and should only be attempted by extremely experienced and perhaps professional aquarists. A Yellow-Edged Moray will basically attack anything that moved.

Chapter 3 – Spiny Eels

The three spiny eels typically kept by aquarists are the Tire Track, Fire, and Peacock Eels. All are nocturnal, and all like to bury themselves in the substrate so the use of soft sand is recommended with these species.

As inhabitants of slow moving rivers, they do not like a lot of water motion in a tank. They tend to be gentle toward other tank inhabitants, but aggressive toward their own kind (with the exception of the Peacock Eel.)

Tire Track Eel

The Tire Track Eel, (*Mastacembelus armatus*), like others in the *Mastacembelidae* family, is a freshwater fish with an elongated body. It is a nocturnal predator that can reach a maximum size of 2.5 feet / 76.2 cm. For this reason, you will need a minimum tank size of 50 gallons / 189.3 liters for this species.

The body of the Tire Track Eel is covered with dark, irregular markings against a lighter, tannish background. The pattern runs from the top of the back to the belly and extends down the entire length of the fish. The dorsal and anal fins are enlarged and the tail flattened.

In creating an environment for a Tire Track Eel, use a soft substrate to allow the creature to safely indulge its habit of burying itself (uprooting your plants and decorations with abandon in the process!) This species will get along well

Chapter 3 – Spiny Eels

with other eels, but should only be kept with larger fish that it won't see as potential food.

This is a carnivore that should be fed live earthworms and black worms. Over time, the eel can be taught to accept frozen bloodworms, krill, ocean plankton, and prepared tablet foods.

Recommended water parameters include:

- pH: 6.8-7.2
- KH 10-16
- Temperature: 72-82 F (22.2-27.7 C)

Since these eels may be as small as 3 to 6 inches / 7.62 to 15.24 cm at purchase, they are relatively inexpensive, ranging from $12 / £7 on the small side up to $40 / £24 for a specimen as large as 10 inches / 25.4 cm.

Fire Eel

The Fire Eel (*Mastacembelus erythrotaenia*) is another elongated freshwater fish of the *Mastacembelidae* family. It has numerous spines on the dorsal fin and for this reason is sometimes simply called the "Spiny Eel."

Like others of its kind it is a nocturnal predator, requires a soft sand substrate to allow it to safely bury himself, and is an escape artist. A tight lid is a must for this fish!

Fire Eels are dark brown to grey, with the body several

Chapter 3 – Spiny Eels

shades darker than the belly. Red stripes and spots mark the body in lateral lines varying in intensity based on age and condition. Juveniles have yellow to amber markings that become deep red with age. The anal, pectoral, and dorsal fins are also edged in red.

In the wild, Fire Eels can grow as large as 3.9 feet / 1.2 meters, but typically in an aquarium setting to not get bigger than 22 inches / 55 cm. Still, they need a fair amount of water with 50 gallons / 189 liters the recommended minimum. Unlike other spinal eels, they do not mind brisk water movement.

- pH: 6.8-7.2
- KH 10-15
- Temperature: 75-82 F (23.8-27.7 C)

At purchase, Fire Eels are generally 4-6 inches / 10.16-15.24 cm and cost around $35 / £20.85.

Half-Banded Spiny Eel

Other Common Names: Belted Spiny Eel, Large Spiny Eel

The Half-Banded Spiny Eel (*Macrognathus circumcinctus*) is a small spiny eel with a long, pointed snout. Adults reach a maximum length of 8 inches / 20.32 cm and so can be kept in a 35-gallon / 133-liter tank.

They are indigenous to Asia, including the Mekong Basin, Thailand, the Malay Peninsula, Sumatra, and Indonesia

Chapter 3 – Spiny Eels

where they live in moving waters and streams with sandy bottoms and dense vegetation.

Note that this species is often confused with the Tire Track Eel, but this creature does not have a diamond-shaped pattern, but rather roughly vertical markings. The result is indeed a banded appearance.

The background color is cream to light brown overlaid with a series of irregular dark patterns that are bold on the upper two-thirds of the body. The markings narrow toward the belly, however and may or may not meet on the lower portion of the body.

The species is nocturnal and very reclusive, burying themselves in the substrate by day. Half-Banded Spiny Eels will do well in a community tank with fish too large to fit in the eel's mouth. Fish under 2 inches / 5.08 cm are at risk.

They are carnivores, however, and will not take to flaked foods, preferring a diet of life and fresh frozen fare. Good options include earthworms, bloodworms, black worms, and brine shrimp.

Feed your Half-Banded Spiny Eel when the tank lights have been turned off for the night, typically 2-3 times per week.

Suggested water parameters include:

- pH: 7.0-7.5
- dGH 5-15
- Temperature: 75-82 F (23.8-27.7 C)

Chapter 3 – Spiny Eels

Half-Banded Spiny Eels are generally sold at a length of about 6 inches / 15.24 cm for $20 / £11.98 or less.

Peacock Eel

Other Common Names: Siamese Spiny Eel

The Peacock Eel (*Macrognathus siamensis*), reaches a length of 12 inches / 30 centimeters in the wild, but stays around 6 inches / 15 centimeters when kept in an aquarium, making it one of the more popular of the spiny eels in the hobby.

This eel is dark brown on the back with light brown flanks and a lighter belly. A fine yellow line runs from the snout down to the caudal fin. Five eyespots are dotted down the dorsal fin and end on the caudal fin. Colors and patterns vary geographically and to some minor degree individually.

In the wild, Peacock Eels are found living on the bottom of densely grown and slow moving rivers and streams in India, Sri Lanka, Thailand, Sumatra and Malaysia. The preferred diet for captive specimens is live worms, bloodworms, brine shrimp, crustaceans and mosquito larvae.

Recommended minimum tank size is 20 gallons / 75 liters with the following water quality parameters:

- pH: 6.0-8.0
- dH 10

Chapter 3 – Spiny Eels

- Temperature: 73-82 F (23-27.7 C)

The Peacock Eel's peaceful nature makes it perfect for a community tank with like-sized, good-natured companions including others of its own kind. When first introduced to a tank, the eel will hide most of the time. It likes lots of plants and sheltered spaces created with PVC pipes, rocks, wood, and roots.

At purchase Peacock Eels are typically 2-4 inches / 5.08-10.16 and cost around $10 / £5.96.

Chapter 4 – Eel-Like Fish

The following creatures all qualify as "eel-like" fish due to their elongated bodies. They are often called "eels," but this is a reference to appearance only. Some are tiny freshwater creatures, others are large marine animals.

Wolf Eel or Carpet Eel Snakelet

The saltwater Wolf Eel is one of about a dozen species in the family *Congrogadinae*, all of which have elongated bodies and are often referred to as "snakelets." For this reason many people find it much less confusing to use the name Carpet Eel Snakelet for this fish.

Wolf Eels are brown or green marked in varying degrees with lighter blotching or mottling. They have the ability to change coloration to match their background as a means of camouflage and self-defense. The strong jaws create a pronounced underbite that helps the fish to crush clams, sea urchins, mussels, crustaceans, and fish.

It is an easy fish to keep, showing good disease resistance, and may be housed in a reef aquarium of 50 gallons / 189 liters or more with a tight-fitting lid.

Be aware, however, that Wolf Eels will eat smaller fish and crustaceans. A proper diet for a Wolf Eel includes meaty fare like small marine fish, chopped clams, and prawns.

Recommended tank mates include squirrelfishes, soldierfishes, angelfishes, butterflyfishes, surgeonfishes and rabbitfishes as well as the more placid morays. It is best not to keep more than one Wolf Eel at a time, as conspecifics will fight.

By nature the Wolf Eel is curious and friendly, rarely displaying aggression, but capable of biting painfully. In the wild they reach a length of 80 inches / 203 cm and a weight of 41 lbs. / 18.6 kg.

Their native range is in shallow seagrass beds, lagoons, and tidal rubble flats from Nicobar Island in the Indian Ocean to Papua, New Guinea on the east, south to northwestern Australia, and north to Ryukus.

With Wolf Eels, be sure to provide ample hiding places, use a tight-fitting lid on the tank, and maintain stable water parameters including the following ranges:

Chapter 4 – Eel-Like Fish

- pH of 8.1-8.4
- sg 1.019 to 1.025
- temperature 74-82 degrees F / 23.3-27.7 C

At purchase Wolf Eel may range in size from 6 inches / 15.24 cm to 14 inches / 35.56 cm and up. They grow to a maximum length of 18 inches / 45.72 cm. Depending on size at sale, prices range from $30-$50 / £18-£30.

Kuhli Loach

The Kuhli Loach is a bottom dwelling, nocturnal, scavenger indigenous to Indonesia, Malaysa, and Java. Its eel-like body is yellow to salmon pink and banded in half circles of dark brown or black stripes.

Since the eyes are hidden within one of these stripes, they are not clearly visible. The mouth turns at a downward angle and is flanked by 3 pairs of barbels used to taste.

Chapter 4 – Eel-Like Fish

Kuhli Loaches are shy fish, preferring to hide in the roots of plants, among rocks, or in caves and driftwood. They are extremely peaceful, and get along well in a community tank at a pH of 6.0-7.0 and a temperature of 75-85 F / 24-29C. They enjoy living in schools of 3 or more of their own kind.

Fully grown, a Kuhli Loach will not measure more than 3-5 inches / 8-11 cm in length and can be easily kept in a 20 gallon / 27 liter covered tank. Use sand or smooth stone for substrate. Note that they can be negatively affected by sudden water changes.

Kuhli Loaches are carnivorous and should be fed frozen and live foods including tubifex and freeze-dried bloodworms. With training and patience, this fish will also eat flake foods.

At purchase, a Kuhli loach will measure 1.5 to 3 inches / 3.81 to 7.62 cm. With correct care, they can live as long as 10 years. Individuals should cost around $3/ £1.79.

Note that the Kuhli Loach and the following loach species (Java, Panther and Weather) can all be kept together without any fear of aggressive behavior.

Java Loach

The Java Loach is similar in size and temperament to the Kuhli Loach but is "unbanded," showing a uniform red-brown or milk chocolate color that can range to near black. The belly is pale and the fins are translucent.

Chapter 4 – Eel-Like Fish

The Java Loach enjoys being part of a school of three or more, and likes hiding places and soft substrate. Adults do not grow larger than 3 inches / 7.62 cm. They are native to Vietnam, Laos, Cambodia, Indonesia, Java, Sumatra, Borneo, and the Malay Peninsula.

Also a peaceful and hardy fish, you can purchase Java Loaches for $3/ £1.79

Panther Loach or Platinum Line Loach

The Panther Loach, native to Pakistan, Northern India, Bangladesh, Myanmar, Nepal, and Thailand also reaches a maximum length of 3 inches / 7.62 cm. It inhabits shallow, slow water in canals and floodplains as well as in swamps and peats.

This fish prefers sand or small gravel for a substrate and needs multiple hiding places and should be kept in a school of at least three. It will eat sinking pellets and good quality flakes as well as thawed bloodworms or brine shrimp.

Recommended water parameters include:

- pH 6.5-7.5
- dH 5
- temperature 72-79 F / 22-26 C

The Panther Loach is peaceful and easily kept. They are generally easy to locate and sold in an affordable range of $3-$5 / £1.79-£2.98.

Chapter 4 – Eel-Like Fish

Weather Loach or Dojo Loach

Weather Loaches are common to the rivers, lakes, and ponds of Asia, although they are also farm raised as aquarium fish and as feeder fish. They, like others of their kind, are bottom dwelling scavengers that live very well in community tanks and should be kept in schools of 3 or more.

The smooth body is gold or pink and the trademark loach barbels or "whiskers" are present around the mouth. The Weather Loach enjoys a planted aquarium and requires 30 gallons / 113 liters or more. It is peaceful and tame to the point of accepting hand feeding.

They are carnivorous and should not be placed with small invertebrates like Ghost or Japonica Amano Shrimp. Appropriate foods include freeze-dried bloodworms and tubifex as well as other types of meaty fare. Recommended water parameters include:

- pH 7.0-8.0
- dh 12
- temperature 50-77 F / 10-25 C

Due to their ability to survive colder temperatures, the Weather Loach can also be used as a pond fish. The name "Weather Loach" is in recognition of the species' reaction to changes in the barometric pressure, which causes them to become agitated and active.

Chapter 4 – Eel-Like Fish

They can survive in poor water conditions by swallowing air from the atmosphere, which is passed through the gut for oxygen extraction before being expelled through the anus.

At purchase, most Weather Loaches are 2-4 inches / 5.08-10.16 cm, but adults can grow to 9-10 inches / 22.86-25.4 cm. They are very inexpensive, selling for around $2 / £1.19.

Note: There are several species of loaches with elongated bodies that qualify under the broad definition of "eel-like" fish. The ones listed here are some of the more common favored by aquarists, but other varieties are available from time to time. All are peaceful, and easily kept.

White Ribbon Eel or Ghost Eel

In the wild, divers most often see the White Ribbon Eel or Ghost Eel at night. It is primarily white with black spots on the head and face, and long nostrils that protrude from the nose. (The body darkens to light brown as they age.) The maximum adult length is 3 feet 4 inches / 1.016 meters.

When kept in an aquarium, the species requires a minimum 50-gallon / 189.27 liter tank with lots of live rock for cover. Use a tight-fitting lid. This eel can work through the tiniest space. Do not place them with aggressive, overly active, or territorial tank mates. The eel is the one that will suffer.

Chapter 4 – Eel-Like Fish

Recommended water parameters include:

- pH 8.1-8.4
- sg 1.020-1.025
- temperature 72-78 F / 22.2-25.5 C

Ribbon Eels can be housed with filter feeder, polyps, soft corals, and mushrooms, but avoid small shrimp, which the eel will eat.

They are nocturnal predators and should be offered live foods as well as freeze-dried krill, uncooked chunks of shrimp, and other meaty food.

At purchase, Ribbon Eels are generally 18-24 inches / 45.72-60.96 cm long and cost approximately $40 / £23.83.

Chapter 4 – Eel-Like Fish

Rope Fish

The Rope Fish is an unusual creature with its elongated body, flat head, and thick, bony scales. In the wild, it lives in standing or slow moving water and gulps oxygen from the surface to survive.

It is a peaceful fish with a curious nature and a great deal of personality. Although it can seem reclusive and reserved, this is only because its eyesight is so poor. In truth, this is a social creature that likes to be with its own kind. Keeping a pair of Rope Fish is highly recommended.

Provide them with a heavily planted tank with plenty of roots or driftwood for hiding. Use a fine gravel or sand for substrate and make sure the aquarium has a tight fitting lid.

The maximum adult length for this species is roughly 3 feet / 0.9 meters, so a 50-gallon / 189.27-liter tank will be necessary. Suggested water parameters include:

- pH 6.0-7.5
- KH 8-22
- temperature 72-82 F / 22.2-27.7 C

Rope fish are carnivores and should be given live food as well as chopped meats (beef heart is good) insect larva, tubifex, bloodworms, and earthworms.

At purchase Rope Fish are typically 8-10 inches / 20.32-25.4 cm in length and cost around $30 / £17.87.

Chapter 4 – Eel-Like Fish

Electric Eel

The Electric Eel (*Electrophorus electricus*) grows quite large in its native waters in South America. The IUCN Red List rates the eels "least concern" thanks to their wide distribution in the Amazon and Orinoco river basins. There, the eels attain a maximum length of 8 feet / 2.43 meters and weigh as much as 45 lbs. / 20 kg.

In captivity, however, Electric Eels are typically no larger than 4-5 feet / 1.21-1.52 meters. They are long-lived fish, often surviving 15 years.

Adapted to life in murky waters, they use the low end of their electrical generation capabilities (about 10 volts) to navigate and as radar for hunting. When they actually want to kill prey, however, they can produce up to 600 volts, enough electricity to stun a fully grown horse.

The eel's orange throat and deep emerald eyes are a striking contrast to the gray / green body covered by small scales edged with teeth on the outer edges. Juveniles will be mostly olive brown with some yellow spotting.

The Electric Eel has an extremely long anal fin beginning near the pectoral fin, but there is no dorsal fin. The small tail fin merges with the anal fin in a continuous line, with the entire structure capable of undulating forwards and backwards.

Although a bottom dweller, the Electric Eel must go to the

Chapter 4 – Eel-Like Fish

surface every 10 minutes to gulp air through a vascularized respiratory organ located in the mouth. It is via this mechanism that the eel takes in approximately 80% of its required oxygen.

Because Electric Eels are hardy by nature, the primary challenges for the aspiring aquarist are spatial and safety based. Clearly this eel can be extremely dangerous and typically will only be seen in zoos and public aquariums.

If kept privately, they should only be acquired by knowledgeable aquarists with years of experience and the proper equipment.

Since juveniles grow quickly and at a steady rate, the minimum recommended tank size is 200 gallons / 757 liters for a single adult with some larger specimens requiring as much as 540 gallons / 2,040 liters. To house more than one Electric Eel a 2,500 gallon / 9,463 liter tank would be needed.

Note that regardless of tank size, the water level should be kept around 6 inches / 15.24 cm from the top to allow the eels to surface and take in air. Specific water parameters for the species are:

- pH: 6.0-8.5
- Hardness: 1-12 dGH
- Temperature: 75-85°F (23.8-29.4°C)

Part of the danger Electric Eels represent is their tendency

Chapter 4 – Eel-Like Fish

to become extremely tame. They are intelligent, and come to associate their keepers with food, rising to the surface to be fed.

This behavior can lull the aquarist into a dangerously complacent mindset. Never attempt to feed an electric eel by hand! The risk of shock is too great!

Electric Eels are carnivores, and will consume almost any smaller creature that will fit in their mouths. In the wild they dine on invertebrates, fish, and small mammals.

Juveniles will do well on insect larvae and worms, but adults require live fish. Over time, however, it is possible to acclimate Electric Eels to a diet of dead freshwater fish, smelt, liver, and similar foods.

Purchase Information: Because it is illegal to own an Electric Eel in many states in the United States and in areas of Europe, and due to their rarity in the hobby, no estimated price was available at the time of this writing.

Chapter 5 – Miscellaneous Eels

The following creatures are, in my opinion, worthy of mention, but do not fit neatly into broad categories to facilitate ease of discussion like the eels or eel-like fish previous discussed. They may be rare in the aquarium hobby, or have highly specific and unique husbandry requirements.

The Purple Spaghetti Eel

The Purple Spaghetti Eel (*Moringua raitaborua*) is a tropical freshwater species native to India, Nepal, Bangaladesh, Indonesia, the Philippines and adjacent areas. In the wild it lives in rivers and estuaries, attaining a maximum length of 17.32 inches / 44 cm.

The eels are rare in the aquarium hobby and are highly reclusive when they are kept in a tank, either remaining hidden or buried in fine sand substrate most of the time.

The name "spaghetti" is well taken for the species. The creature's head is so small it's almost indiscernible from the rest of the body. Even the eyes, which are covered with skin, are barely visible.

The overall color is a pink to purple brown. Both the dorsal and anal fins, located far back on the body, are folds joined with the caudal fin creating the look of a "paddle" extension. For this reason, you will sometimes see this creature called the Pink Paddletail Eel.

Chapter 5 – Miscellaneous Eels

The Purple Spaghetti Eel is a carnivore, but due to its small size presents no real threat to the vast majority of creatures typical to community aquariums. Since it lives in estuaries, it does equally well in freshwater or brackish environments. The projected lifespan is 5-12 years.

Purple Spaghetti Eels will not take flake or tablet foods, but should be fed live fish, shrimp, and worms on a daily basis. Their preference is for nocturnal feeding. Tubifex and bloodworms also work well with the species, as do brine shrimp.

The recommended minimum tank size is 30 gallons / 113.56 liters to afford the creature sufficient room to burrow. For aquarists with a love of exotic specimens, this is a perfect species, although difficult to find and certainly not recommended for beginners.

Purple Spaghetti Eels require well-oxygenated, clean water with changes of 30% per week. The ideal environment is a slightly acidic (pH 8.1-8.4), mid-level brackish tank with specific gravity of 1.005-1.010 maintained in a temperature range of 72-78 F / 22.2-25.6 C.

The Rubber Eel

The Rubber Eel (*Typhlonectes natans*) is also called the Sicilian Worm. It is a limbless amphibian native to Columbia that reaches a maximum length of 18-22 inches / 45.72-55.88 cm. The body is dark gray to black.
These hardy creatures will eat almost anything that cannot

Chapter 5 – Miscellaneous Eels

escape them. In the wild they live on insects, spiders, and worms, but in an aquarium will eat pellet food and pieces of shrimp or fish.

Since Rubber Eels are nearly blind and locate their food by taste and smell, they will not go after feeder fish and can be easily kept in the same tank with small, active species.

Rubber Eels require a soft substrate and enjoy caves and other objects that create spaces for hiding. They need a clean, well-aerated tank with a tight cover. Specific water parameters include:

- pH 6.5
- temperature 74-78 F / 23.3-25.5 C

Rubber Eels are relatively rare and when you can locate them, expect to pay $60-$75 / £35.75-£41.71 per individual.

The Spotted Garden Eel

The Spotted Garden Eel (*Heteroconger hassi*) is not that difficult to find, but all too often dies quickly as it require a highly specialized environment to thrive. It is a tropical fish indigenous to shallow waters in the Pacific and Indian Oceans and the Red Sea.

(Also note that this species has a reputation for not shipping well. For this reason, many vendors will not guarantee live arrival or offer money back on unsuccessful shipments. The estimated mortality rate for Garden Eels

Chapter 5 – Miscellaneous Eels

that do survive shipping and are placed in a correct environment is still a staggering 75%.)

Spotted Garden Eels live in colonies, and do best in captivity in groups of 3 or more, with 6-10 eels being the ideal allowing for 1 square foot / 0.09 square meter of open sandy substrate per eel.

The spaces should be contiguous (sharing common borders) to allow the eels to replicate the colony they would create in the wild. This need will put a serious constraint on other elements of aquascaping in the tank.

Given the space requirements, expert hobbyists who have kept the creatures recommend a minimum tank size of 120

Chapter 5 – Miscellaneous Eels

to 180 gallons / 454.25-681.37 liters. The necessary water parameters are:

- ph 8.1-8.4
- sg 1.020-1.025
- temperature 72-78 F / 22.2-25.5 C

The maximum length for the species is 16 inches / 40.64 cm, but in captivity rarely exceeds 11 inches / 27.94 cm, which means the substrate should be around 12 inches / 30.48 cm in depth.

The eels feed with half of their body length extended, but they retract entirely inside their burrow for protection or when the tank lighting is off.

(Be sure to use a coarser quality of sand for the top half inch / 1.27 cm of the substrate so the material doesn't shift around with the water's motion. Additionally, this anchoring of firmer sand will help the eels to remain upright to feed.)

Because Garden Eels derive their nutrition from floating zooplankton, they are completely safe to include in a reef tank. It's best, however, not to mix them with aggressive carnivorous species as tank mates or with big, active fish that will scare them.

If Garden Eels remain in their burrows too much of the time, they won't get enough to eat and will suffer the negative consequences of stress.

Chapter 5 – Miscellaneous Eels

Garden Eels remain anchored in their burrows while they feed, limiting their reach to only a few inches. The current in the tank must be run gently across the sand around their burrows and must be adjusted if the eels decide to relocate. When a colony is correctly established, it will look like waving seagrass.

Food must be placed in the path created by the pump's flow to deliver it to the eels. Prawn, fish, and oyster eggs as well as red cyclops work well with this species as do live brine shrimp.

At purchase, Garden Eels are 3-7 inches / 7.62-17.87 cm in length and cost approximately $35-$40 / £20.85-£23.83.

The Marble Swamp Eel

The Marble Swamp Eel (*Synbranchus marmoratus*) is not a true eel, but a large fish with an elongated, slender body. It is, in the terms of the hobby, a "tankbuster."

They will basically eat anything that comes into their path, and dig so aggressively in the substrate that an undergravel filter is not an option with the species.

Marble Swamp Eels are, however, incredibly hardy, and can live in deplorable water conditions and have no issue with brackish water. The creatures are native to South America, ranging from Mexico to Argentina.

As adults, they reach a maximum size of 5 feet / 1.52

Chapter 5 – Miscellaneous Eels

meters. Because they are solitary and aggressive to the point of belligerence, no more than one should be kept at time in a tightly secured tank.

Marble Swamp Eels are carnivores, and will eat a wide range of meaty foods. It is difficult to put a price to them as they are most often sold individually among enthusiast communities and kept for their sheer novelty.

American Eel

The American Eel (*Anguilla rostrata*) is native to the eastern Coast of North America. It is catadromous, meaning, in this case, that the creatures migrate from fresh water into the sea to spawn. In the case of the American Eel, however, the migration is place specific, with spawning occurring in the Sargasso Sea.

Chapter 5 – Miscellaneous Eels

The eels are olive green with brown shading to greenish yellow with light gray or white shading. A long dorsal fin runs from the middle of the back and flows into the ventral fin. There are no pelvic fins, and only small pectoral fins near the midline.

The species is occasionally kept by aquarists, and are easy to maintain so long as the tank is tightly secured. By day the eels tend to remain buried in the substrate or hiding under rocks, emerging at night to engage in restless activity.

They are so curious, they will get into all kinds of trouble, swimming into filtration tubes and getting caught in filters. They are not, however, sensitive to water conditions and will eat almost anything.

The downside to keeping the species in activity is that the creatures will reach a maximum adult size of 5 feet / 1.52 meters. At that point, they can't be kept with smaller fish and have to be moved to solitary tanks or euthanized.

Releasing them into the wild isn't an option since this practice could disperse pathogens among the wild population in local rivers in lakes.

There are laws governing the capture of this species when they are small, but larger specimens can be netted in virtually any stream on the Atlantic or Gulf Coasts.

Chapter 5 – Miscellaneous Eels

Again, this is an "eel" species kept mainly as a novelty and due to their availability for wild capture in a clearly defined region.

Chapter 6 – Creating Aquatic Environments

If you are already an aquarist, deciding to keep eels will be a matter of matching the species you select to the population of your tank or of designing a new tank with these creatures in mind. Your decision-making process may well be based solely on the eel or eels in which you are interested.

For beginning aquarists with an interest in eels, the process is somewhat different. You may be fascinated by one of the larger saltwater morays, but far too inexperienced to take on a major tank of 100 gallons / 378.54 liters or more. For this reason, I'd like to talk about some of the basic considerations involved in the design of any aquarium habitat.

Weight Matters – A Lot!

For newcomers to the hobby of aquarium keeping, the two most common mistakes are going too small or thinking too big. With true eel species, erring on the side of a small tank is a mistake you must avoid at all costs. These creatures grow quickly and are adept escape artists. If you start out with an undersized tank, you'll be starting *over* in a matter of months.

Do not, however, swing to the opposite extreme without a clear understanding of this simple principle: *the greater the volume of water in your tank, the more it will weigh*.

Chapter 6 – Creating Aquatic Environments

Say, for instance, that your recommended minimum tank size for an eel is 150 gallons / 567.81 liters. You then go shopping for a custom tank (often a necessity at these greater volumes) and decide to go with 180 gallons / 681.37 liters to give your eel some growing room.

A 180-gallon / 681.37 liter tank will weigh 1,440 lbs. / 653.17 kg!

Now, granted, you can do a lot with that much water. The standard rule for aquarists is 1 inch / 2.54 cm of adult fish per 5 gallons / 18.9 liters of water. In a tank of that size, you can stock up to 36 inches / 91.44 cm of fish.

Most of the saltwater moray species, however, grow to lengths of 3 feet / 0.9 meters or more, which takes care of your 36 inches / 91.44 cm in one swoop.

But, you reason, eels are bottom dwellers and the tendency is generally toward overstocking a tank. "I can get away with more, right?" Sure, unless you moray likes to eat small fish.

Some aquarists will put no more than eight carefully chosen aggressive fish together in a 360 gallon / 1362.75 liter tank, which would weigh 2,880 lbs. / 1306.56 kg. That's 1.44 American tons!

What Can Your Floors Take?

Can the floors in your home take that kind of weight

Chapter 6 – Creating Aquatic Environments

without being reinforced? The residential standard for weight bearing in the United States is 40 lbs. (18.4 kg) per square foot for a "live load," which is defined as the weight of everything you add to the home when you move in, including furniture, bookshelves, the people themselves, and your planned aquarium.

The theory is that the live load is spread uniformly over the entire floor when considered from wall to wall. It is not a rating for a maximum load positioned in any given area. So, this information, easily obtained from an Internet search, can also lead aquarists to make very **bad** decisions about the placement of their tanks.

The real issue is **NOT** the weight bearing capacity of the floor, but the structures that lie beneath the floor. Clearly, the best place for a really large aquarium is directly on a concrete "slab on grade." For most homeowners, that would mean placing the tank in the basement.

The next best place is over the top of a column or bearing wall, but this is often complicated by the fact that those structures are already supporting added weight – like the second floor of your home! How do you decide on the strongest room?

Finding the Strongest Room

Go into your basement and look up at the floor joists. Wherever the joists cover the shortest distance is the room with the strongest framing underlying the floor. Wherever

Chapter 6 – Creating Aquatic Environments

the joists are the longest is the weakest room. If possible, go with the room that has the strongest floor.

If that isn't possible, put your tank as close to a load bearing column or wall as possible in a position perpendicular to the floor joists so that the weight is distributed out over the joists themselves. An aquarium stand designed with a bottom continuous runner distributes the weight of the water more evenly than a stand with four legs.

Is That All I Need to Know?

Absolutely not! I have given you just enough information to either make you dangerous, which was not my intent, or to illustrate that this is a complicated question for which there are NO easy answers, NO quick fixes, and NO universal formulas.

If you are going to get a tank this large, hire a structural engineer or an aquarium design firm to come in and determine the best location in your home to place the tank.

Do not be surprised if structural modifications are necessary to support the weight of your tank safely OR if you have to alter your plans to keep a species of eel in favor of something smaller.

If you are looking at a saltwater eel species you will also find out quickly that there are different kinds of saltwater tanks. Deciding on the safest place to put your aquarium may limit your size choices, but that is only the first of

Chapter 6 – Creating Aquatic Environments

many decisions ahead of you.

Tanks by Type

The major saltwater configurations are: fish only, fish only with live rock, and reef. Each has specific requirements for setup, maintenance, stocking, and management.

- Fish Only (FO) aquariums are designed to house marine fish with little if any cosmetic embellishment beyond artificial coral. This is a good option for a first-time marine aquarium to allow a "newbie" to learn about water chemistry, equipment, and population management.

- Fish Only with Live Rock (FOWLR) tanks are a bridge between an FO tank and a reef tank. Live rock is included, specifically coral reef fragments that house natural colonies of marine life like various invertebrates, sponges, and nitrifying bacteria. The rock is not only aesthetically beautiful, but an important secondary means of filtration.

- Reef Tanks are challenging environments that may include only a few fish, but an abundance of coral and invertebrates. The sensitivity of these creatures to water condition creates a high-level challenge in perfecting chemically stable water paired with correct lighting.

Chapter 6 – Creating Aquatic Environments

Although freshwater tanks are arguably less expensive and less difficult to maintain, all tanks require an understanding of basic water chemistry.

The Basics of Water Chemistry

Water quality should be an area of the aquarium hobby about which you become almost obsessive. You are, after all, in charge of the atmosphere in which your fish will live and breathe. It is an almost godlike responsibility, and one that can result in a veritable underwater apocalypse if you allow your tank to become a toxic soup.

There are several basic measurements with which you must become familiar, and about whose interaction you must develop a fundamental understanding. These include, but may not be limited to the following.

pH

The acronym "pH" stands for "power of hydrogen" and is a measurement of hydrogen ions.

- The more ions in the water the lower the pH number and the greater the acidity of the water.

- The higher the pH number, the greater the water's alkalinity.

The greater the stability of the pH, the better. Fish do not do well with rapidly or constantly changing pH values.

Chapter 6 – Creating Aquatic Environments

Water Hardness

There are two measurements you will see associated with water hardness: GH and KH. The first is a measure of calcium and magnesium ions and generally not an issue for average hobbyists.

KH measures bicarbonate and carbonate ions and is an expression of how alkaline the water is, or what is its capacity to neutralize acid. Water with a stable chemical composition registers a higher KH value.

You will also encounter "dH" which is a measure of "General Hardness" based on dissolved calcium carbonate. Water with a dH of 0-4 is very soft; 20 or more is very hard.

Most species can survive wide ranges of water hardness, but this measurement can be important in creating correct breeding conditions for some fish.

Specific Gravity

Specific Gravity describes the relative salinity of water. The only way to get a true measure of salinity is to allow the water to evaporate and then to weigh the salt residue. Enthusiasts instead use a hydrometer or refractometer to arrive at an "sg" number.

An added complication is the fact that the salinity of natural seawater varies by location in a range of 1.020 to 1.030. Given this fact, saltwater aquarists typically strive to

Chapter 6 – Creating Aquatic Environments

maintain an sg reading of 1.022, but this can change slightly by tank type.

For instance, FO and FOWLR tanks need an sg of 1.020-1.025, while a reef tank falls in the range of 1.023 to 1.025.

Clearly these are precise measurements that require constant monitoring and adjustment. When you become an active aquarist, you also become a water chemist whether you want to be one or not – and I have discussed only the most basic measurements!

Thankfully, you will have a range of water testing equipment at your disposal, including test kits and a new generation of digital and electronic meters, including some tied to real-time computer systems.

While this approach to water quality may seem over the top, consider your investment in several hundred dollars worth of fish, which can be wiped out in a matter of hours by a simple electrical outage. Truly serious saltwater enthusiasts typically have standby generators for just such emergencies.

Cycling: Establishing Viable Water

All new tanks must be "cycled" to make the water acceptable to sustain life in the closed environment of the tank. Adequate amounts of beneficial bacteria must be in place to control the build up of ammonia, created by waste materials, and convert it to harmless nitrate, or the water

Chapter 6 – Creating Aquatic Environments

itself will kill your fish.

There are several methods for establishing this critical bacteriological food chain, but essentially it's a "with" or "without" fish proposition.

A traditional method is to select a species that can tolerate toxic levels of ammonia, like damselfish, toss them in the tank, and hope for the best. This is, however, arguably quite cruel and has given rise to "without fish," chemical based alternatives.

Regardless of the method chosen, the ultimate goal is to create water with nitrate levels below 10 parts per million. (With some species of eels, less than 3 parts per million is optimal.)

Dispelling the Major Myth

Just in case I have to come right out and say it -- you can't just buy some fish – or eels – toss them in a tank full of water, and expect them to thrive!

Far too often small tanks are an impulse buy and it's only after the fact that people realize – if they care to go to the trouble – that maintaining an aquatic environment is serious business.

Clearly for experienced aquarists, most of this chapter falls under the heading of "preaching to the choir." I am speaking mainly to those people who have simply seen a

Chapter 6 – Creating Aquatic Environments

large tank, spotted an eel in that tank, and decided, "Wow! It would be cool to have one of those."

Sure it would be cool, but there's a tremendous amount of work involved *first* and most true eel species need seriously large tanks. Do not get involved in this hobby if you cannot afford good equipment or if you are not willing to take the time to learn about and to create a proper environment.

Chapter 7 – Creating and Keeping a Moray Tank

Within the aquarium hobby itself, aquascaping has become its own art form. The skill is akin to gardening underwater. The goal is to create functional and artful landscapes with plants, coral, rocks, stone, and other structures that are not only beautiful, but life enhancing for the creatures whose world is defined by the boundaries of the tank walls.

In deciding how to discuss creating an "eel" tank, I have decided to take most of the "eel like" fish "off the table." In their profiles, I provide information on water parameters and discuss personality. Most, like the various loaches, don't require anything special beyond the normal concerns relative to population management in any tank.

No serious aquarist ever buys a fish of any type on a whim and just tosses it in a tank to see how it does. Throw a docile fish in with big carnivores, and they'll thank you for the snack.

For the most part, the special considerations that relate to the highly popular moray species also apply to other forms of eels, so I will use them as the benchmark for talking about habitat design.

Form and Function

It would be a mistake to think of aquascaping for any species as simply "interior decorating." Certainly the arrangement of tank elements in a way that is pleasing to

Chapter 7 – Creating and Keeping a Moray Tank

the eye is important, but the selection of plants or live rock is not merely a matter of aesthetics, but also an aspect of habitat management.

Both plants and/or live rock serve as a means of natural filtration to maintain water quality and to support the tank's bacteriological food chain. Often living material in an aquarium is chosen for some role it plays in the habits and behavior of organisms within the population.

Some species of fish, for instance, will not thrive unless they have grass and plants to use as a hiding place. Most eels are not happy without rocks and caves in which they can hide by day.

To successfully aquascape a tank, you must understand the basics of water chemistry, the selection and use of substrates, the control of temperature and lighting, and the basic principles of design. With a species as needs specific as eels, a fair amount of engineering acumen is not out of order.

Eels are muscular, powerful creatures. They like to burrow in the substrate as well as hide within tank structures. Many will infiltrate working mechanical parts if these areas are not adequately shielded. Structures that are not sturdy or well anchored are no match for a determined eel.

Moray Habitats

If you are of the "go big or go home" school of thought and

Chapter 7 – Creating and Keeping a Moray Tank

are determined to have one of the larger moray eels, the first aquascaping decision – the size of your tank – will be determined by the species you choose to acquire.

You will certainly be working to control some behavioral knowns. Morays are:

- escape artists
- have a tendency to eat their roommates
- topple rocks and structures with abandon
- hate too much light
- can be aggressive or finicky eaters

All of these "knowns" are more easily managed in a tank that is the appropriate size for the eel in question (preferably with room to spare.)

All eels are escape artists, so a secure tank with a lid to prevent daring escape leaps is a must. The following rules of thumb for space requirements are good guidelines, but you should do species-specific research for any eel you plan to house.

One good way to do this is to join an aquarium discussion board and simply say, "I'm thinking of keeping a Snowflake Moray Eel. Any suggestions on aquascaping?"

Such forums are an excellent resource for "real world" advice from enthusiasts who have already tried certain arrangements and have a sense of what does and does not work with the species you're considering.

Chapter 7 – Creating and Keeping a Moray Tank

If you do not have a species in mind and are still trying to select an eel, consider the following rough approximations:

- Species that grow to an adult length of 3-5 feet / 0.91-1.52 meters need aquariums from 55-180 gallons / 208.2-681.4 liters.

- Species of less than 2.5 feet / 0.76 meters can be housed in 20-30 gallon tanks / 75.7-113.5 liters.

- So called "mini morays" that never grow beyond 15 inches / 38.1 cm can be kept in 10-15 gallon / 37.85-56.78 liter tanks.

Volume vs. Configuration

Don't make the mistake of thinking that volume alone determines a tank's suitability to serve as a home for a large species of Moray. Considerations of height trail a distant third to length and width.

If you are going to keep a creature that reaches a maximum adult length of 24 inches / 0.6 meters, you want your tank to be long enough for the eel to stretch out completely.

The recommended rule of thumb is that an eel tank be twice the length of the creature it will house. Therefore, if you have a 24 inch / 0.6 meter eel, the tank should be, at minimum, 48 inches / 1.21 meters in length and as wide as possible.

Chapter 7 – Creating and Keeping a Moray Tank

Eels are bottom dwellers. If a moray cannot stretch out and move about normally, the level of resulting stress will greatly decrease its projected lifespan.

There are additional considerations relative to volume, however. Moray eels are messy eaters and they produce a great deal of waste. Any tank in which they are housed must have good biological and mechanical filtration, including a protein skimmer to improve overall water quality.

The greater the volume of water in the tank, the more biological wastes will be able to dissipate, meaning fewer water changes for you – although you will still do more water changes weekly keeping an eel than almost any other aquatic species.

Finally, adequate tank volume paired with the correct physical configuration will cut down markedly on instances of aggression.

A standard 180-gallon / 681.4-liter aquarium's dimensions are typically:

- 72" L X 24" W X 24" H
- (182.8 cm x 60.96 cm x 60.96 cm)

Depending on the material chosen (glass or acrylic), the tank alone will cost $675 - $1250 / £404.32 - £748.75.

Chapter 7 – Creating and Keeping a Moray Tank

Glass vs. Acrylic

The glass vs. acrylic debate is ongoing in the aquarium hobby. Many purists say glass, period. There are, however, some "pros" for going with acrylic, including:

- lighter in weight
- resistant to cracking
- easier to cut holes into to customize plumbing
- can be molded into more interesting configurations
- provides better insulation

On the flipside, however, acrylic also:

- scratches easily
- costs more
- changes appearance over time
- needs increased support

For many people, the decision boils down to one of budget and personal taste as well as weight. An acrylic tank weighs roughly half as much as the glass equivalent *before* the water goes in.

Lighting

Correct lighting is crucial to reducing stress with the moray species. If you go with fluorescent lighting, opt for blue-actinic bulbs that create a dawn/dusk effect. This can be used in combination with high-intensity bulbs to simulate a day/night cycle, or solo for a "deep" water effect. Since

Chapter 7 – Creating and Keeping a Moray Tank

lighting will affect all living creatures in the tank, take the needs of the entire population into consideration.

Mercury-vapor lighting can create the rippling look of creatures resting under moving surf, but these lights do generate more heat. They can be good to create areas of deep shadow in the tank, but may not be appropriate for the moray species that inhabit shallow waters.

Metal-halide lights broadcast powerful, full-spectrum light and really bring the colors of a tank to life. While perfect for reef tanks, the truth is that these lights are simply too intense for the light sensitive eyes of most eels.

The strength of the bulbs push the eels into deeper hiding, so if you do go with this lighting type, make sure your eels have really deep and dark spaces into which they can withdraw.

Temperature

On average, moray species thrive in a temperature range of 72-80 F / 22.2-26.6 C. You cannot, however, put the heater in the tank with moray eels.

They are far too curious for their own good, and will expose themselves to superficial burns by bumping at the unit at night, especially if it has any kind of indicator light.

The best option is to place the tank heater in the sump to bring the water up to a uniform temperature as it circulates

Chapter 7 – Creating and Keeping a Moray Tank

through the display tank. This strategy basically saves the eels from themselves!

Substrate

The selection of substrate is highly dependent on the species you are keeping. I will diverge from the "moray middle ground" approach here and strongly stress the need to research the preference of any species of eel or eel-like fish you are considering keeping.

Some of these creatures like to burrow in substrate, so for them, sand is the best option. Others that hide among rock and coral on living reefs really don't need any other substrate.

You want to both cater to the preference of the eel species, and select a substrate that will not clog up your filters intakes, which is often a problem with very fine sand.

Some experts recommend crushed coral substrate exclusively for morays. As the material breaks down, it naturally elevates the tank's pH and serves as a continuous buffer. Guarding against sudden and often fatal swings in pH levels is an important aspect of eel husbandry.

Tank Structures

Never underestimate the reclusive nature of a moray eel, or the creature's real physical need for a sense of security. Stress is an ongoing concern with morays.

Chapter 7 – Creating and Keeping a Moray Tank

Create sheltering sites large enough to accommodate the eel's entire body throughout the tank. Morays can be highly discriminating when it comes to shopping for "real estate," so give them a lot of variety. Make the holes both large and small, as some eels really like to wedge themselves in tight spaces.

Design structures that are both attractive and tough enough to withstand your moray's habits, including burrowing. Simply stacking rocks or corals is not enough. You will need to drill holes and anchor the items, generally with nylon zip-ties, to achieve the proper level of stability.

You can also use clay pot halves and lengths of PVC pipe to create caves and tunnels, just be sure to select pipe large enough to accommodate a *fully-grown* eel. Consider the option of burying the PVC pipe under the substrate to provide even greater privacy for your eel.)

Use your imagination to create custom accommodations for your eels, but be cautious about leaving small gaps anywhere. Eels are not only prone to escape, but can injure themselves seriously if they get caught in a structure and struggle to work free.

Observe your eel's behavior and demeanor to determine if the amount of shelter available is right for the animal's needs. Eels that feel overly exposed are restless or listless by turns. They may refuse food, show an increased rate of breathing, and swim erratically through all layers of the tank rather than remaining on the bottom.

Chapter 7 – Creating and Keeping a Moray Tank

Security Precautions

All moray eel species need to be housed in tanks with heavy, tight-fitting glass lids, often referred to as "canopies." Typically these units are hinged in the middle with a handle that faces toward the front of the tank. Be aware that you may have to have a lid manufactured for a larger aquarium.

If there are any holes cut in this lid to accommodate hoses, intake stems, or piping, they must be absolutely *exact*. If necessary, bring such openings down to size with nontoxic sealant (silicon, hot glue, or spray-on foam), but do not allow *any* gaps through which an eel can push its head.

If the gap is half the width of the eel's head, the creature will be able to force itself through.

Do not be surprised if you have to weigh the lid down, or secure the lid in place with fasteners on the sides. Eels can be incredibly determined!

Water Quality and Health

Moray eels thrive in water with a specific gravity that falls in the range of 1.018 to 1.024. There should be no detectable levels of ammonia and only traces of nitrate, less than 3 ppm. Maintain pH levels 8.0 and 8.4. The perfect water temperature is 74-80 F / 23.3 - 26.6 C

Disease is rarely an issue, but eels do sometimes suffer from

Chapter 7 – Creating and Keeping a Moray Tank

an infestation of nematode worms, detectable as raised, moving books under the skin.

Eels are sensitive to copper compounds and to organophosphates used to treat various diseases. Also, some morays have been known to develop skin lesions from coming into contact with fiberglass.

Older specimens can suffer from skin tumors, or develop cloudy eye (which also occurs in the wild), but overall these are hardy animals if they receive the correct care.

On rare occasions a moray may also suffer from skin tumors, and older specimens may develop cloudy eyes, a condition I have seen in both wild and captive eels.

Feeding Time

Moray eels put on quite a show at feeding time, viciously ripping and tearing into their meal with teeth bared. There is a tendency in the hobby to overfeed morays for this very reason; they're far too interesting to watch.

If you are tempted to do this, remember that the more you feed your eel, the more bio-waste goes into the water. Since pristine water quality already demands frequent water changes for eels, anything that makes this ongoing problem worse is a *bad* idea.

I am often asked just how many water changes are necessary with eels and my standard answer is, "How ever

Chapter 7 – Creating and Keeping a Moray Tank

many you have to do to keep the water parameters chemically stable."

The number of changes will be different for every tank and circumstance, but I can promise you whatever the schedule may be, overfeeding your eels will double it!

Never give your eels any food that has been dyed or colored, contains preservatives or seasoning, has been salted, or in any way is artificial, cooked, blanched, or "fake."

Another reason to avoid overfeeding is the fact that morays eat before they think, to the point that excess food in the gut will back up into the throat leading to inflammation, irritation, bloating, and possibly infection.

On average, morays eat once a week, although this may vary by species. Concentrate on high-quality, meaty foods offered in variety to guard against nutritional deficiencies. In each of the eel profiles in this book, I have recommended potential foods for the animal in question.

Although many morays will only accept live food, it's a good idea to transition them to fresh and thawed foods as quickly as possible. Feeding live also adds bioload to the tank because morays don't "clean their plates." There will be lots of "parts" left over that add tremendous amounts of pollution o the tank.

There is also a very good argument for moving morays off

Chapter 7 – Creating and Keeping a Moray Tank

live foods as quickly as possible to dull their predatory instinct in regard to other tank inhabitants. If you are attempting to keep a moray with fish, even large aggressive ones capable of taking care of themselves, the last thing you want is the eel eyeing his next-door neighbors as potential lunch fare.

Truthfully, Morays have poor vision, but an excellent sense of smell. Especially in a community tank setting where there is competition for the meal, it's a good idea to use a feeding stick to put the food directly in front of the eel's nose.

The feeding stick is really nothing more than an elongated skewer, but you can also use long feeding tongs for the same purpose.

Some people opt to teach their eels to take food directly from their keeper's hands. While this is absolutely an intriguing spectacle, and no doubt entertaining for the aquarist, let's not lose sight of the fact that moray eels have a lot of teeth – sharp ones.

The eel cannot distinguish where its supper ends and your fingers begin, so this is truly an ill-advised and foolish risk.

Most experts are in agreement that a moray eel's diet should be supplemented with a broad-spectrum vitamin as a boost not only to the creature's immune system, but as a way to keeps its color and stress coat intact. Vitamin supplementation also helps to stimulate the appetite and

Chapter 7 – Creating and Keeping a Moray Tank

balance the metabolism.

The best means of delivery is to soak food items in a multivitamin mixture obtained from your aquarium store before offering the item to your eel.

Issues of Pure Aesthetics

I have had many beginning aquarists tell me that aquascaping simply eludes them. They cannot create an underwater landscape that is both aesthetically pleasing and functional, and this is a source of great frustration – and usually expense.

With that in mind, I will offer just a few universal design principles that apply equally to all tanks (or for that matter to just about any "decorating" project.)

The Golden Ratio

The Golden Ratio has been around since the time of the Greeks and is a mathematical ratio for creating the most pleasing arrangement to the human eye. Basically, it calls for placing the focal point of a scene off center forcing the viewer's eye to wander back and forth.

Personally, I just eyeball this placement, but here's the formula.

- Measure the length of your tank and divide the number by 2.618.

Chapter 7 – Creating and Keeping a Moray Tank

- Use the result to measure from one end of the tank toward the middle.
- Where the tape measure stops is the place you should position your focal point.

After you've done this a few times, you'll get an eye for the ratio and will start using it naturally.

The Rule of Thirds

The "Rule of Thirds" is derived from the Golden Ratio. Imagine your tank divided into nine equal squares forming a 3 x 3 grid.

Place significant elements on the lines or where the lines intersect at the four points in the center of the grid.

Merge this concept with the idea of primary and secondary points of interest in a tank placed in the foreground, middle, and background.

The interplay of these regions, and their transition one into the other, can create eye-catching depth and detail.

Don't feel that every inch has to be packed. Open space, when planned for dramatic effect is also a powerful design element, and one that is true to nature.

Avoid the Symmetry Trap

Avoid the symmetry trap in aquascaping your tank.

Chapter 7 – Creating and Keeping a Moray Tank

Matching up everything of equal size on opposite sides of the tank looks contrived and unnatural.

I sometimes refer to this as making an "underwater doll's house." Remember that you are trying to recreate a natural environment, one where *asymmetry* creates the beauty.

Some books that may be of help to you include:

- Takashi Amano – Nature Aquarium World: How You Can Make a Most Beautiful Aquarium
- Peter Hiscock – Creating a Natural Aquarium
- Robert M. Frenner – The Conscientious Marine Aquarist
- Alf Jacob Nilsen and Svein A. Fossa – Reef Secrets
- John H. Tullock – Freshwater Aquarium Models
- John H. Tullock – Saltwater Aquariam Models
- Jeff Senske and Mike Senske – The Inspired Aquarium: Ideas and Instruction for Living with Aquariums

Clearly with eels, your primary goal is to meet the needs of the creatures themselves, but you also want to set them off to their best advantage in the tank. It is almost impossible for a visitor not to be interested in an aquarium with an eel in residence.

Chapter 8 – Health Considerations

Eels can bounce back from almost any kind of disease, but they are sensitive to medications, chemical pollutants, and unstable water quality. When an eel becomes stressed from any of these causes, they can weaken and become ill. If addressed quickly, however, eels have a good record for near miraculous recoveries.

It is imperative that you maintain stable water. A pH shift of even 2/10-3/10s of a point can seriously stress an eel, with even more dramatic shifts causing fatal "pH shock." It's also important to avoid nitrogenous poisoning caused by high levels of ammonia, nitrites, and nitrates.

The higher the quality of the water in your tank and the more careful your maintenance of the environment, the healthier your eels will be.

That beings said, the first procedural "healthcare" task you face in keeping an eel (or even an eel-like fish) is to make sure that the creature is appropriately quarantined and then transitioned to your main tank.

Although the following description is for a saltwater tank, the same steps also apply to a freshwater scenario.

Introductory Quarantine

When you first acquire your marine eel, the individual should be placed in a quarantine tank for a period of 3-4

Chapter 8 – Health Considerations

weeks. During this period, the eel will display agitation and will be highly stressed. Both jumping and powerful swimming are likely behaviors. Be extremely cautious about repeated escape attempts during this period.

Float the bag in which the eel arrives in the quarantine tank for half an hour to equalize the temperature. Then pour .5 cup / 0.12 liter of water from the quarantine tank into the bag every half hour for three hours and add a small air stone.

After three hours have passed, release the eel into the quarantine tank. When it is time to transfer the creature to the display tank, repeat the same procedure.

For the first few days in both the quarantine and display tanks, use only dim lighting, returning to the regular lighting, feeding and cleaning schedule after three days.

If your eel does get out of either tank and lands on the floor, use a wet towel to pick it up. Be gentle! Rinse off anything stuck to the eel and replace the eel in the tank.

It's rather shocking how well eels bounce back after being out of the water even for several hours, but avoid this kind of incident at all costs!

External Parasites

Some of the external parasites than can infest moray eels include flatworms, hookworms, leeches, and protozoa. All

Chapter 8 – Health Considerations

are bloodsuckers, but they normally do not have the capacity to penetrate an eel's mucous covering known as the "slime coat." Weakened or stressed individuals are, however, more vulnerable to attack.

External parasites are, easily recognized and treated. The eel will be listless, refuse to eat, and scratch endlessly against anything it can find.

The skin will typically show evidence of the parasites, which may appear as small black or white spots, blotches, or even worms.

The level of infestation will be strongest around the head, throat, and gills due to increased blood flow in those regions.

When parasites are detected, remove the moray from the display tank and place it in fresh water for 10-12 minutes, which will cause the majority of the parasites to turn loose and fall off. If necessary, repeat the freshwater dip a day or two later.

Next, move the moray to a quarantine tank that contains one drop per gallon / liter of 37% (approximately 200 ppm) of Formalin.

Over the next 7-10 days, change 40-60% of the water in the quarantine and display tanks daily to disrupt the lifecycle of any remaining parasites. The eel should remain in the quarantine tank under observation for at least a month.

Chapter 8 – Health Considerations

White Spot or Ick

White Spot disease, often called "Ick" occurs very commonly and is simple to diagnose and treat. Essentially your eel will look as if it's been dusted in salt. The white spots are actually ciliated protozoa that attach themselves to the eel's skin. They drop off into the tank's substrate where they reproduce, spreading rapidly.

Remove the eel from the tank and place it in a quarantine tank with 1 drop of 38-42% Formalin per gallon. (Remove all activated carbon for the duration of the treatment.)

A freshwater dip can also be used for severe cases. Although the parasites are relatively easy to kill, they leave behind open sores that are vulnerable to secondary infections.

Keep the water in the quarantine tank in pristine condition, conducting 50-60% water changes daily for 3-4 weeks. Also increase feedings to help the eel regain its strength.

To rid the display tank of the parasites, change 50-75% of the water daily for 8-10 days. This will disrupt the lifecycle of the protozoa. Siphon the substrate carefully with each cleaning, but do not use any kind of chemical to treat the display tank.

Wash all of the non-living tank apparatus in very hot water 90 F / 32.2 C to kill any protozoa that have permeated the items.

Chapter 8 – Health Considerations

Internal Parasites

It is quite rare for a moray eel to be affected by internal parasites, but they can fall victim to various protozoa, cestodes, nematodes, and acanthocephalans. It may be necessary for a marine veterinarian to examine a blood or stool sample to confirm the diagnosis.

Symptoms of internal parasites may include: any extreme change in appetite, weight changes, labored breathing, color changes, or protruding parasites in the mouth, nares, or anus. Some parasites, notably nematodes, will be visible as tiny swimming worms in search of even more hosts in the tank.

The three medications used most commonly for internal parasites are Fenbendazole, Piperazine, and Metronidazole. Clearly the eel should be removed to a quarantine tank with all forms of carbon and filtering agents taken away.

The dosage will vary by medication used and parasite present. Again, the services of an expert may be required. A vet may indicate the need for medicated foods to be offered to the eel, give specific recommendations for water changes, and take periodic blood and/or fecal tests.

The quarantine period will last 3-4 weeks in most instances, although stubborn cases may need longer.

Chapter 8 – Health Considerations

Injuries

In truth, your eels are more likely to suffer from self-inflicted injuries that can range from simple bruises to actual lacerations thanks to their nosy behavior and escapist tendencies. Deep cuts often leave scars, but in some cases wounds heal slowly and become infected.

These kinds of injuries are much easier to *prevent* than to treat. Do everything you can to construct and maintain your environment in a way to both stop escapes before they start, and to protect your overly curious eels from injury.

It's also important not to make sudden moves near the tank that will frighten the eel, or to startle the eel by flicking strong lights on at odd times of the day. This sort of thing easily sends an eel crashing into the side of the tank or other structures.

Be especially vigilant about tight spaces into which the eels can become caught, or any edges that are rough or irregular that can inflict cuts. Also make sure the eel has plenty of places to shelter and hide. If they are feeling insecure, they will rub their noses raw looking for a deeper hideaway or retreat.

If a physical injury does occur, remove the eel to a quarantine tank and observe the creature closely until the abrasion heels. As always, superior water quality is a must. If infection does set in, erythromycin is an excellent choice for a wide-spectrum antibiotic.

Chapter 8 – Health Considerations

Fungal and Bacterial Infections

Fungal and bacterial infections typically develop as a secondary infection associated with a trauma or injury. The evidence will appear as rough, bloody, irregular patches of skin. Fungus may manifest as areas of rot, skin discolorations, or a milky film covering the entire body.

As with all other health problems, the eel should be immediately quarantined and treated with erythromycin, or in the case of fungal infections, with Furan. If the infection is going to respond well to treatment, signs of recovery will be evident in 24-36 hours.

Malnutrition

Malnutrition in eels is almost always traceable to a lack of variety in the animal's diet. The eel's level of activity diminishes, its color fades, and more and more time is spent hiding.

Increasing the range of foods offered easily solves the problem. Do not cook or blanch any of the items. Both diminish the nutritional value of the diet.

Vitamin deficiency and malnutrition lower an eel's growth rate, lead to decreased energy, and can cause developmental malformations. Over the long term, a poor diet will significantly reduce an eel's captive lifespan.

One rather dramatic indication of malnutrition (as well as

Chapter 8 – Health Considerations

stress or poor water quality) is slime shedding. To some extent this is a natural and daily phenomenon, but large patches of discolored, exposed skin is a warning sign of a larger problem.

Since the "slime coat" is an eel's first line of defense against disease and parasites, excessive mucous shedding should never be ignored or dismissed.

Tumors

There are two kinds of tumors typically seen in eels: subcutaneous growths and deep tissue lesions. Tumors that appear as discolored lumps just under the skin can often by removed by a specialist, but deep tissue tumors are almost

Chapter 8 – Health Considerations

always fatal.

The deeper tumors may be caused by internal scar tissue that grows to such an extent it places pressure on a nerve or an organ, or the mass may be a malignancy. Symptoms may include violent lashing of the tail, dramatic respiratory changes, and the appearance of writhing in agony.

By the time this level of discomfort is evident, the eel is likely in the end stages of the disease and euthanasia is the only humane option.

Euthanasia

The most merciful means of putting the eel out of its suffering is to place it in the freezer in a container filled with water. As the water freezes, the eel's systems slow down and the animal falls into a deep sleep until its heart stops. The process is completely painless.

Chapter 9 – Frequently Asked Questions

Although I recommend reading the entire text to get a real idea of the work involved in acquiring and caring for eels and eel-like fishes, these are some of the most commonly asked questions.

Are eel aquariums a lot of work?

Keeping any aquarium, especially one that is primarily designed to showcase a highly specific creature like a moray eel, is definitely a labor of love. It demands careful creation of eel-appropriate structures and superb water quality.

Smaller "eel-like" fishes that can be more easily integrated into existing tanks do not pose the same kind of challenges, but care still must be taken to create the correct population mix.

If keeping an eel of any sort is something you love, the work you put into its husbandry will be a pleasant and absorbing passion – one shared by many people. There are, in fact, more aquariums in homes in the United States than there are dogs and cats.

The important thing is that if you have never kept an aquarium, or never had an eel, you place education first. Don't make your mistakes on living creatures. Learn everything you need to do to create an eel environment and set everything up well in advance of actually buying the eel

Chapter 9 – Frequently Asked Questions

itself. Also, realize that this is a highly species-driven decision. Some eels are no longer than your finger, while others achieve lengths of 3-4 feet / 0.91-1.22. Clearly, the extremes in required equipment alone will be considerable.

Can I really keep a moray eel?

Yes, but the viable selection is relatively small due both to the size and level of aggression you will see in these species. There are about 200 moray eels, of which only five can be safely put in a tank with other fish, and then only according to strict population guidelines. These include:

- Dragon Moray Eel
- Snowflake Moray Eel
- Zebra Moray Eel
- Whitemouth Moray Eel
- Chainlink Moray Eel

All of these eels are carnivores with a menacing appearance, and will not do well with other fish unless they have plenty of room and are fed correctly.

It sounds like eel tanks are really big. Will that create a lot of humidity in my house? What about possible water damage?

Any aquarium is subject to evaporation, which is why most truly big tanks are outfitted with an auto top off system to maintain the correct volume of water. The evaporation is not enough, however, to really elevate humidity in your

Chapter 9 – Frequently Asked Questions

home, or even in the room where the tank is kept.

An overflow box is always a good idea with large aquariums to contain leaks, or in the case of eels, to even potentially contain the creatures themselves. Eels will try almost anything to escape, so good tank security is absolutely essential.

As to the potential for water damage, discuss the option of a rider with your insurance agent. This is a specific addition to your policy that would cover damage relative to tank failure or overflow.

Why is tank size such a big deal with eels? Won't they just stay small if I put them in a small tank?

No. The myth that any fish only grows according to available space is absurd. All fish have a maximum physical length and a recommended minimum tank volume.

For eels, that's twice their adult body length. If you are going to get a creature that can, in captivity, reach a length of 5 feet, you will need a 10-foot / 3.05-meter tank.

Just how hard are eel tanks to manage?

The hardest part in keeping a tank for eels is maintaining perfect, *stable* water chemistry. Eels are incredibly sensitive to sudden shifts in water quality and can often die if this critical aspect of husbandry is not handled carefully and

Chapter 9 – Frequently Asked Questions

well.

Beyond that, maintaining a well-varied diet, constructing correct levels of shelter, and keeping proper lighting conditions are all of equal importance.

Population management must be carefully planned to avoid predation, but that's generally a matter of preventing the eel from eating its neighbor.

What do I have to consider in terms of tank location?

In terms of tank placement, think about the weight of the tank. A gallon of water weighs 8 lbs. (3.628 kg), so a 180-gallon (681.37-liter) tank will weigh 1,440 lbs. or 653.17 kg.

Placing any tank in front of a window is not a good idea because the water will not only become too warm, but you'll get uncontrolled algae growth.

Additionally, controlling lighting conditions is extremely important with eels. Most species kept as pets are nocturnal and will not react well to bright lights.

Where is it safe to put a big tank in my house?

A 100-gallon (378.54 liter) tank can be placed just about anywhere, but from 100 to 220 gallons (378.54 to 832.79 liters), the tank should sit along a load-bearing wall perpendicular to the floor joists.

Chapter 9 – Frequently Asked Questions

For tanks of 220 to 400 gallon (832.79 to 1514.16 liter), reinforced floors will likely be necessary. At volumes above 400 gallons (1514.16 liters) the tank must be placed directly on a concrete slab.

How much electricity does a big tank use?

To get an accurate calculation, you will have to keep actual usage records that reflect your local cost of electricity and the efficiency of your equipment. Using LED lights will certainly cut down on costs, but these lights may not be right for eel species.

On average, a 90-gallon tank (340.687 liters) uses 400-600 watts per day for the essential equipment, with the lighting adding another 200-700 watts. (These calculations can, however, vary widely.)

Should I buy a glass tank or one made of acrylic?

As a rule of thumb, aquariums 300 gallons (1,135 liters) and under are built of glass. The material is cheaper, and these tanks tend to come in standard "off the shelf" sizes and configurations.

From 300 gallons and up, tanks are typically custom designed and made of acrylic. The material is lighter and clearer, but it is expensive, and does scratch more easily. Acrylic is, however, more flexible in terms of fabrication.

Afterword

As I said in the opening chapter of this book, I have somewhat broadened the use of the word "eel" for the purposes of this discussion to include many species of "eel-like" fish with elongated bodies.

The true marine eels, primarily the morays, have a chapter of their own as well, and they are clearly not fit dwellers for just any home tank. Many attain adult lengths of 3-4 feet / 0.91-1.22 meters.

In composing the text, I struggled to strike a balance between existing enthusiasts wanting to add an eel to their tank, and beginners passionate about creating a new environment around a showcase eel specimen. Frankly, I think some of the most useful information is in the profiles of the species I've included.

I think you have to "window shop" for your eel and make all of your subsequent plans from there. You may greatly admire one of the big morays, but lack the time, space, and money to create a massive tank that in the end might house only the eel and one or two tank mates.

Many aquarists opt for smaller eel-like fishes because they get the look of an exotic, elongated tank inhabitant without all the extra husbandry complications. This was my own introduction to "eels" as a child when my Dad brought home several Kuhli loaches to serve as part of his "live cleaning crew."

Afterword

Because eel-like fishes are not substantially different from other fish, most of the specifics of eel husbandry address the needs of true eels – nocturnal and often aggressively carnivorous creatures that are, paradoxically, highly sensitive to: water quality, chemical contaminants, diet, and lighting.

Hopefully I have achieved a good survey of what it means to keep eels as a hobbyist and, in the Relevant Websites section, provided you with ample additional sources to pursue the direction, and the creature, you find most intriguing.

I will not even claim to have listed all the types of eels and eel-like fishes that are kept in tanks by enthusiasts. As I was assembling my research, it seemed as if I was always stumbling on to a forum post somewhere by a person describing yet another type of rare eel they managed to acquire and were attempting to keep successfully.

The species listed here are the most common, but be prepared to encounter an "odd ball" out there with a "for sale" tag. Be careful! Population management is crucial with eels, and they almost never come out the losers.

Regardless of the size or type of eel you opt to put in your tank, these are intriguing creatures with fascinating habits and high visual appeal. They will quickly become a topic of attention and discussion in your tank, and they will certainly never be boring. For one thing, you'll never know

Afterword

at just what moment your eel may decide to make a break for it!

If there is any one thought with which I would leave you, it is this. Do not put an eel in an undersized tank! Pay attention to the recommendation of minimum tank size and go larger if at all possible.

Eels will become highly stressed in cramped quarters, and will often sicken and die from that one factor alone. If you go stir crazy in small spaces, you may be able to empathize with the creature's feelings.

No pet, certainly not one as exotic as an eel, should ever be adopted on a whim. If, however, you are capable of providing an aquarium eel with the standard of care it needs and deserves, you'll never regret adding one of these "water serpents" to your tank.

Relevant Websites

The following reference sites are provided for your further research and study. All were extant at the time of this writing in mid-2014.

Eel-Specific Links

FishChannel
www.fishchannel.com/fish-species/saltwater-profiles/snowflake-moray-eel-2.aspx

Saltwater Fish
www.saltwaterfish.com/product-snowflake-eel

WikiPedia - Moray Eels
www.en.wikipedia.org/wiki/Moray_eel

National Aquarium - Wolf Eel
www.aqua.org/explore/animals/wolf-eel

Aquarium Domain - Jeweled Moray Eel
www.aquariumdomain.com/viewSpeciesMarine.php?id=181

Reef Keeping
www.reefkeeping.com/issues/2002-12/fm/

How to Raise Peacock Eels
www.animals.pawnation.com/raise-peacock-eels-3726.html

Relevant Websites

Monterey Bay Aquarium - Wolf Eel
www.montereybayaquarium.org/animal-guide/fishes/wolf-eel

Spotted Garden Eel - Wakatobi
www.wakatobi.com/fishID/species_profileS.php?photoID=11

Critter Hub - Blue Ribbon Eel
www.critterhub.com/saltwater/blue-ribbon-eel-care/

Australian Museum - Whitemouthed Moray
www.australianmuseum.net.au/Whitemouth-Moray-Gymnothorax-meleagris-Shaw-Nodder-1795/

ReefBuilders - Ribbon Eels Spawning
http://reefbuilders.com/2010/04/17/documented-spawning-ribbon-eels-steinhart-aquarium/

General Aquarium Links

"How to Start Your First Saltwater Aquarium: An Interview with Even from Colorado."
www.petfishtalk.com/interviews/saltwater/saltwater.htm

The Aquarium 101 - Your Aquarium Info Center
www.theaquarium101.com/tips-keeping-saltwater-fish/

Successfully Set Up a Saltwater Aquarium - Melev's Reef
www.melevsreef.com/overview.htm

Relevant Websites

Reef Aquarium Forum
www.reefland.com

Fish Channel - All Saltwater Species
www.fishchannel.com/fish-species/saltwater_all_landing.aspx

Fishlore - Aquarium Fish Information
"Saltwater Aquarium Fish Guide for Saltwater Fish"
www.fishlore.com/SaltwaterBeginners.htm

Saltwater Aquarium Online Guide
www.saltwater-aquarium-online-guide.com

Beginner Saltwater Invertebrates
www.saltwateraquariumsupplies.org/beginner-saltwater-invertebrates

A Beginner's Guide to Setting Up a Large Marine Tank
www.fishkeeping.co.uk/articles_29/large-marine-tank-setup.htm

Corals for Your Saltwater Aquarium: A Photo Guide
www.idiotsguides.com/static/quickguides/pets/corals-for-your-saltwater-aquarium-a-photo-guide.html

Reef Cleaners - Beginner's Guide
www.reefcleaners.org/index.php?option=com_content&view=article&id=46&Itemid=59

Relevant Websites

LiveAquaria (Supplies and live fish.)
www.liveaquaria.com

The Top 10 Worst Tank Busters
www.ratemyfishtank.com/articles/146

Setting Up a Saltwater Aquarium
www.petco.com/caresheets/fish/SetUpSaltwaterAquarium.pdf

Setting Up a Freshwater Aquarium
www.petco.com/caresheets/fish/SetUpFreshwaterAquarium.pdf

Creating a Brackish Habitat Fish Aquarium
www.fishchannel.com/setups/special/creating-a-brackish-habitat.aspx

Water Chemistry
www.aquariuminfo.org/water.html

BlueZoo Aquatics
www.bluezooaquatics.com/productDetail.asp?did=1&cid=17&pid=620

Fish Data Base
www.fishbase.org

Glossary

A

acidity - The pH level of the water is one of the most common quality measurements taken. It is not as crucial as the amount of toxic ammonia present in a tank, but is a variable that should be monitored and kept within the recommended range.

actinic lights - These blue spectrum lights use fluorescent bulbs to recreate the quality of ocean light at a depth of approximately 30 feet. Although there are other kinds of lights now commonly used in saltwater tanks, actinics are still typically used in reef tanks.

activated carbon - This is an absorbent carbon-based material used in filtration systems. Activated carbon will not remove either ammonia or nitrite, nor does it work to soften the water. It is useful, however, in the control of organic matter in the water.

air pump - The generic term for the devices used in any type of aquarium that serve to aerate or oxygenate the water.

algae scraper - As the name implies, this is a tool that facilitates the mass removal of algae growth from the glass or acrylic sides of an aquarium.

Glossary

algae - The catch-all term "algae" covers an extensive collection of aquatic plants that proliferate as nuisance growth in aquariums.

alkalinity - This somewhat confusing measurement refers to the capacity of water to act as a buffer. The measurement addresses the ability of the water to neutralize acid without creating a dip in pH levels.

ammonia - This is the major and most deadly toxin that accumulates in aquarium water as a consequence of fish excrement. Ammonia must be neutralized by the establishment of the nitrogen cycle in the tank, a life cycle of beneficial bacteria working in concert to create water capable of sustaining marine life.

anoxia - A state in which no oxygen is present.

aquaculture - The practice of cultivating aquatic lifeforms as a source of food or for pleasure.

aquascaping - The aesthetic arrangement of elements in an aquarium including the selection of inhabitants, with a goal of creating an authentic underwater environment.

aquarist - The keeper of an aquarium.

aquatic plant - Any plant that will grow fully or partially submerged in water.

Glossary

B

beneficial bacteria - Bacteria introduced into an aquarium through the establishment of the nitrogen cycle that work to convert toxic ammonia into relatively harmless nitrate.

benthic - Living in or occurring in the bottom level of a body of water or in an aquarium.

C

carbonate hardness - The measurement of water's ability to absorb and neutralize acid. One of the important factors of water quality in an aquarium.

carbon dioxide (CO_2) - The respiration of animals and plants (during photosynthesis) creates this odorless, colorless gas.

chiller - A device in an aquarium's life support system that function to lower water temperature.

chlorination - To make water safer for human consumption, municipal water systems add the purification agent chlorine. Only de-chlorinated water should be used in aquariums.

cycling - In cycling a tank, beneficial bacteria are established to work in the nitrogen cycle for the purpose of converting toxic ammonia to nitrates, thus rendering the water capable of supporting marine life.

Glossary

D

deionization (DI) - During this process, water is purified by the use of ion exchange resins working with activated carbon and a bacterial filter. The system removes 100% of inorganic chemicals.

detritus - Any dead material of a bacterial, plant, or animal nature, which, through bacterial processes, can be degraded.

E

ecosystem - A community of organisms interacting with the physical environment which they inhabit.

F

fluorescent light - Light fixtures used in aquariums to supply low cost, broad spectrum illumination.

G

glass aquarium - Standard sized aquariums routinely sold in pet stores are typically made of glass, while high-volume customized tanks are generally constructed from acrylic.

H

hang on the back filter - As the name implies, a filter hanging off the back of the aquarium outfitted with a draw

Glossary

tube to carry water through the mechanism to be filtered and returned to the tank.

heater - A device for the control of water temperature, typically a glass tube, used in an aquarium. Generally accurate to within 2 degrees of the target level.

herbivore - Animals that eat plants as their staple food source.

hydrometer - A device that is used to determine a fluid's specific gravity or salinity.

I

invertebrate - Aquarium animals lacking spines. Examples might be starfish, clams, worms, and crabs.

L

lateral line - Perforated scales running in a line along a fish's flank that are sensitive to vibrations in the water.

live rock - Rock or coral seeded with marine organisms and used in aquariums as both decorative material and biological filtration. They serve as the focal point of reef tanks.

N

nitrification - A bacteriological process that serves to

Glossary

convert ammonia to nitrate and then in turn changes the nitrite to nitrate.

O

omnivore - Animals that consume both plants and other animals for food.

P

predator - Animals that prey on other animal for food.

R

reverse osmosis (RO) - A process of water purification utilizing high pressure and selective membranes. RO will take out 100% of bacteria and 85% to 95% of inorganic chemicals present.

S

salinity - The level of dissolved salts present in water.

specific gravity - The measurement of the degree of salt present in aquarium water at any give time.

substrate - The material lining the bottom of an aquarium. In saltwater tanks, sand is most often used.

sump - A container or box, usually with a water reservoir attached, that serves as an equipment storage area.

Glossary

T

territorial - An expression of actual or perceptual ownership of a chosen area in the surrounding environment. A behavior exhibited by many marine species.

W

water quality - The chemical composition and stability of aquarium water, and a crucial element of tank husbandry.

Index

Abbott's Moray, 33
aggressive, 13, 15, 18, 19, 21, 22, 24, 63
American Eel, 10, 59
amphibiains, 11
Anuilliformes, 10
aquarist, 62, 98, 110
aquarium, 97
aquarium eels, 12
bacteria, 66
Barred Moray, 32
black worms, 36
Blackspotted Moray, 33
brackish, 108
brine shrimp, 39
carnivorous, 19
Carpet Eel Snakelet, 41
caudal fin, 39
Chainlink Moray, 15, 27, 98
community tank, 17, 40
crustaceans, 21, 23, 24
dorsal fin, 36, 39
Dragon Moray Eel, 15, 17, 98
Dragon Moray Eels, 19
earthworms, 36
eel-like, 10
Electric Eel, 10, 50, 51, 52
Electrophorus electricus, 10
Enchelycore pardalis, 17
European Eel, 10
Fimbriated Moray, 33
Fire Coral Eel, 29, 30
Fire Eel, 36
freeze-dried bloodworms, 44, 46
Ghost Eel, 47
Golden Dwarf Moray, 28, 29
Groupers, 19
Guinea Moray Eel, 25
Guineafowl Moray, 25
Half-Banded Spiny Eel, 37, 38
Hawks, 19
humidity, 98
invertebrates, 66
krill, 36
Kuhli Loaches, 1, 2, 44
Lionfishes, 19
Marble Swamp Eel, 58
Mastacembelidae family, 10, 35, 36
Mastacembelus erythrotaenia, 36
Naked-Backed Knifefish, 11

Index

ocean plankton, 36
Painted Moray, 25
Panther Loach, 45
Peacock Eel, 35, 39, 40
pH, 18, 22, 24, 26, 27, 30, 36, 37, 38, 39, 43, 44, 45, 46, 48, 49, 51, 54, 55, 67, 79, 81, 88, 109, 110
prey, 16, 21, 50, 114
Puffers, 19
Puhi'onio, 25
Purple Spaghetti Eel, 53, 54
refractometer, 68
Rope Fish, 49
Rubber Eel, 54
Rubber Eels, 11
salinity, 68
Salinity, 18, 22, 24, 26
saltwater moray eels, 15
secondary filtration, 66
Snappers, 19
Snowflake Eels, 21
Snowflake Moray Eel, 15, 19, 20, 98
Spaghetti Eels, 10
Specific Gravity, 18, 68
spiny eels, 35, 39
Spiny Eels, 10
sponges, 66
Spotted Eel, 25

Spotted Garden Eel, 2, 55, 106
Spotted Moray, 25
stress, 18, 57, 76, 77, 79, 88, 95
substrate, 35, 36, 114
tank, 1, 2, 3, 4, 12, 13, 17, 18, 19, 21, 22, 23, 24, 25, 26, 27, 30, 32, 33, 35, 37, 38, 39, 40, 42, 44, 47, 49, 51, 53, 54, 55, 56, 57, 58, 59, 60, 62, 63, 64, 65, 66, 67, 69, 70, 71, 72, 73, 74, 75, 76, 77, 78, 79, 80, 81, 85, 86, 87, 88, 89, 90, 91, 92, 93, 98, 99, 100, 101, 102, 103, 104, 107, 109, 110, 111, 113, 115
teeth, 18, 21, 23, 26
temperature, 28, 30, 43, 44, 45, 46, 48, 49, 54, 55, 57, 73, 78, 81, 89, 91, 111, 113
Temperature, 18, 22, 24, 26
Tessalata Moray, 31
Tire Track Eel, 35
Triggers, 19
tubifex, 44, 46, 49
Turkey Moray, 25
water chemistry, 100
Weather Loach, 46

Index

White Ribbon Eel, 47
Whitemouth Moray Eel, 15, 25, 98
Wolf Eel, 41, 42, 43, 105, 106
Worm Eels, 10

worms, 113
Yellow-Edged Moray, 34
Zebra Eel, 23, 24
Zebra Moray Eel, 15, 17, 22, 98

www.ingramcontent.com/pod-product-compliance
Lightning Source LLC
Chambersburg PA
CBHW071709040426
42446CB00011B/1987